chocolate

chocolate

Linda Collister

photography by Martin Brigdale

RYLAND
PETERS
& SMALL
LONDON NEW YORK

Dedicated to Emily, Daniel, and Stevie, with love.

First published in the United States in 2002
by Ryland Peters & Small, Inc.
519 Broadway, 5th Floor
New York, NY 10012
www.rylandpeters.com

10 9 8 7 6 5 4 3 2 1

Library of Congress Cataloging-in-Publication Data

Collister, Linda.
   Chocolate / Linda Collister ; photography by Martin Brigdale.
      p. cm
   Includes index.
   ISBN 1-84172-319-3
      1. Cookery (Chocolate) 2. Chocolate. 1. Title.

TX767.C5 C654 2002
641.6'374—dc21   220202129

Senior Designer Steve Painter
Commissioning Editor Elsa Petersen-Schepelern
Editors Kathy Steer, Jennifer Herman
Production Meryl Silbert
Art Director Gabriella Le Grazie
Publishing Director Alison Starling

Food Stylists Bridget Sargeson, Linda Collister
Stylist Helen Trent
Indexer Hilary Bird

Author's acknowledgments
I would like to thank the following for their help with this book:
Elsa Petersen-Schepelern, Steve Painter, Martin Brigdale, Helen Trent, Barbara
Levy, Bridget Sargeson, Annette and Will Hertz. Thanks to Michelle Kershaw and
Lakeland Limited for baking equipment, Alan and Simon Silverwood of Alan
Silverwood Ltd for loaf tins and baking trays, and Pam Bewley for the Magimix
food processor. Robin Kendal, Michael Levy, Jean-Jacques Bernachon, Sara
Jayne Staines, and Chantal Coady helped me with my chocolate education
(though any mistakes are mine.) And last but certainly not least Alan Hertz.

Notes
•All spoon measurements are level unless otherwise specified.
•All eggs are large, unless otherwise specified. Uncooked or partially cooked
eggs should not be served to the very young, the very old, people with
compromised immune systems, or to pregnant women.
•Before baking, weigh or measure all ingredients exactly and prepare baking
pans or trays. Weighing scales and a set of cup measures are recommended for
use with these recipes.
•Ovens should be preheated to the specified temperature. Recipes in this book
were tested in 4 different kinds of ovens—all work slightly differently. I
recommend using an oven thermometer and consulting the manufacturer's
handbook for special instructions.

contents

the food of the gods ...

For most of its long history, chocolate was a luxury, reserved for privileged people and special occasions. But *Theobroma cacao*—the "food of the gods"—was first appreciated not just for its taste, but for its economic, spiritual, and medicinal virtues.

Wild cacao is native to the lowland jungles of Mexico and Central America, and the ancient Maya people who lived there turned the bitter, inedible seeds of cacao into foamy beverages used in religious rituals. In the Aztec empire, the male elite also used the drink called *xocolatl (*bitter water) in their daily religious rituals, as well as an aphrodisiac and a health tonic.

Although when Columbus "discovered" the New World, he saw cocoa beans, he never tasted them. It was the Spanish conquistador, Cortés, who saw cocoa beans used as currency by the Aztecs and realized their economic value. He introduced the drink to the Spanish court as a medicine, and founded plantations in the new Spanish territories.

For the first hundred years or so its use was confined to the court, nobility, and the Church, but with royal intermarriage, the fashion for chocolate drinks spread throughout Europe. By the time of the restoration of King Charles II in 1660, the English thought of chocolate as a stimulant and medicine, a cure for hangovers, and a source of strength and energy. Then, by the early 18th century, Dr Hans Sloane thought of adding milk and using it as a palatable drink for Queen Anne's sickly children. He sold the recipe to the Quakers, who saw it as a healthy alternative to alcohol.

Although cocoa was once used exclusively to make beverages, we now more often associate chocolate with a solid bar of confectionery. The maker uses a mixture of dried beans, and the flavor of the finished chocolate depends largely on the quality of the beans and the skill of the blender. The king of chocolatiers, Jean-Jacques Bernachon in Lyon, France, uses up to twelve varieties and compares the beans to the *premier cru* wines of Bordeaux.

The flavor of chocolate is also determined by the way the dried beans are roasted, as it is very easy to scorch them. After roasting, the "nibs" are gently crushed to make a paste of minuscule particles. The resulting paste is blended with additional melted cocoa butter, real vanilla, and a little sugar. This mixture is slowly melted and stirred to release the flavors and to give the smoothest possible texture.

The percentage of cocoa solids in the chocolate should be on the label of your chocolate bar. About 60–70 percent is perfect, but a high percentage is not a guarantee of good flavor—the chocolate must be perfectly balanced. It shouldn't leave your mouth feeling greasy or astringent, nor should it have a harsh or burnt aftertaste. It's worthwhile trying several different brands.

Using the best ingredients will make a difference to the taste and quality of any recipe you make. Choose the finest chocolate you can afford and look out for organic and fairtrade brands.

Today, chocolate is an enduring passion for millions of people. It is now known to contain phosphorous, iron, calcium, and theobromine, which affects the central nervous system and acts as an antidepressant. I've heard it said that women feel for chocolate the way men feel for football. I hope you'll love these recipes as much as I do.

techniques

melting chocolate

1 To chop chocolate, use a large sharp knife and a clean dry board (make sure the board doesn't have any lingering odors from chopping garlic or onions).

Put the evenly chopped chocolate into a dry heatproof bowl and set over a saucepan of steaming but not boiling water. The water should not touch the base of the bowl or start to boil.

2 As the chocolate starts to melt, stir gently with a spatula or wooden spoon, so the chocolate will melt evenly rather than in hot spots.

3 When the chocolate has become completely smooth, remove the bowl from the heat to avoid overheating.

Note If the chocolate becomes too warm or comes into contact with a drop of water or steam, it will become stiff and hard rather than smooth and liquid. This is called "seizing" and means that the chocolate is unusable and cannot be saved.

tempering*

1 To temper chocolate, melt it as shown on page 11, then increase the temperature of the steaming water so the chocolate reaches 113–118°F. Stir gently with a spatula, so the chocolate heats evenly. Remove the bowl from the heat as soon as it reaches 113°F, because the chocolate will start to seize if it reaches 122°F. In addition, it may not set to the desired finish and may also develop a bloom (see note opposite).

*Note Tempering means to melt and cool chocolate to make it shiny, smooth, and even in color. In this form, it may be used in many recipes as a frosting or decoration, or in chocolate candy making.

2 Next, the temperature must be reduced to 80°F. This can be done in two ways.

Firstly, by adding chopped chocolate to the bowl. Add about one-quarter of the initial weight of chocolate used, then stir gently with a spatula, so the chocolate melts and lowers the temperature of the chocolate in the bowl to 80°F.

Alternatively, when the chocolate has reached 113°F, put the bowl into a larger bowl filled with cool, not cold, water and stir gently with a spatula until the temperature is 80°F. Make sure no water comes into contact with the chocolate.

3 When ready to use, reheat the chocolate to 84–86°F by setting the bowl over a saucepan of gently steaming water (do not let the base of the bowl touch the water). Stir gently with a spatula and use as soon as the chocolate reaches the correct temperature.

4 To test if the chocolate has been correctly tempered, dip the tip of a clean, dry spatula into the chocolate, then cool and let set. When properly tempered, the chocolate on the upper surface will appear smooth and evenly colored rather than streaky or slightly textured. Peel the chocolate away from the spatula—the underside should be shiny.

Note The larger the quantity of chocolate, the easier it is to control temperatures— about 8 oz. is easy to handle. Any excess can be reset and stored for future use. Pour the excess into ice cube trays, let set, then press out and store in a plastic container.

Bloom If the chocolate is stored incorrectly, either at a very high temperature or exposed to a wide range of temperatures, the cocoa butter starts to crystallize on the surface as dull grey streaks. This is called a "bloom." (It does not affect the flavor.)

dipping and coating chocolate candies

Above To give a smooth, professional finish to a handmade chocolate candy, drop it into a bowl of tempered chocolate (page 12). Lift it out using a round wire tool (left) or chocolatier's fork (right), available through Mail Order Sources and Websites (page 126). Bounce the fork up and down several times on the surface of the melted chocolate so the surface tension pulls off the excess. Use the round wire tool for round chocolates and the chocolatier's fork for any other shape with a flat base.

Put the dipped chocolates onto a baking tray lined with nonstick parchment paper or wax paper and let set.

Above To give a twirled top to round chocolate candies (left), press the round wire tool gently onto the surface of the chocolate, then lift and twirl. To give a ridged top to square shapes (right), drag the prongs of the fork across the surface of the chocolate candy, to leave a striped mark.

Let set. Store in an airtight container in a cool place or in the refrigerator.

making chocolate curls

Chocolate curls and shavings give a professional finish to a cake or dessert.

1 Make tempered chocolate as shown on pages 12–13, then pour the chocolate onto a clean marble slab (this will help to cool the chocolate very quickly).

2 Quickly, before the chocolate sets, use a spatula to spread the chocolate thinly to about 1/16–1/8 inch thick.

3 Keep working the chocolate with the spatula, until it sets and becomes matt and dull rather than shiny.

4 To make the curls, hold a large, sharp knife at an angle away from you and shave the top off the sheet of chocolate, pushing the knife through the chocolate and ending at the far edge. Store in an airtight container in a cool place.

Note The edges may be too thick to make good curls, but keep them and any unsatisfactory attempts—you can melt and reuse them.

making solid molded chocolates

1 Make tempered chocolate as shown on pages 12–13. Use a ladle to overfill the chocolate molds with the chocolate—the molds should be clean, but do not oil or grease them.

2 Gently tap the molds on the work surface to expel any air bubbles.

3 Scrape off the excess chocolate with a spatula to give a completely flat surface. The chocolate contracts as it sets, so it's important to cool the chocolate quickly. Cover with plastic wrap to avoid any condensation, then refrigerate, ideally at 51°F. It will take about 20 minutes to set.

4 To remove, invert the mold over a sheet of nonstick parchment paper or wax paper and tap gently to loosen the chocolate. Store in an airtight container in a cool place.

making hollow molded chocolate shapes

1 Make tempered chocolate as shown on pages 12–13. Use a ladle to pour the chocolate into the clean, unoiled mold.

2 Swirl the mold so the chocolate completely coats the inside of the mold.

3 Pour out the extra chocolate, then scrape the excess from the rim of the mold with a spatula or knife. Set the mold upside down on a baking tray lined with nonstick parchment paper or wax paper and give a gentle tap to expel any air bubbles. Put into the refrigerator and let set for about 20 minutes. Give the mold a second coat of chocolate in the same way as before, then chill until set.

4 When set, lift off the plastic mold. To join two halves of the egg, put the halves back into their molds (try not to touch the tops or the shiny surfaces will look fingered) and, using a pastry bag or knife, pipe or spread a little melted chocolate onto the rim. Press the two halves together and let set in the refrigerator for about 20 minutes before unmolding again. Store in an airtight container in a cool place.

making stippled easter eggs

To make a two- or three-tone egg, use tempered chocolate in at least two different colors—milk, white, or plain.

Above Finger-painted Easter egg (front) and Stippled Easter Egg (rear).

1 Make tempered chocolate as shown on pages 12–13. Use two types of chocolate such as bittersweet and white. Holding the mold by the rim, use a clean, dry sponge to dab the thinnest possible coat of the first coloor chocolate into the mold, then put into the refrigerator and let set for about 20 minutes.

2 Using a ladle, pour in tempered chocolate of a contrasting color.

3 Swirl the chocolate, pour out the excess, then put the mold into the refrigerator and let set for about 20 minutes. Give the mold a second coat of the solid color and let set in the refrigerator.

making finger-painted easter eggs

1 Finger-painting with chocolate gives an abstract finish. Dip your finger into melted tempered chocolate and paint the mold in a speckled design. Put into the refrigerator and let set for about 20 minutes.

2 Repeat, filling in some of the gaps with another color chocolate. Put into the refrigerator and let set for about 20 minutes.

3 Fill the mold with a third color, swirl and tip out the excess chocolate.

4 Put the mold into the refrigerator and let set for about 20 minutes, then add a second coat of the same color and let set. The eggs can be joined together with melted chocolate (see page 17).

chocolates

Handmade chocolates are the best of indulgences—just one perfect chocolate can make anyone feel special, and a box of handmades will make a terrific gift. Each brand of chocolate has slightly different characteristics—try out several to find the one you prefer. Store the finished chocolates in an airtight plastic container in the refrigerator, and eat at room temperature.

chocolate dials

5½ oz. bittersweet chocolate

1 recipe praline (page 30)

⅓ cup large seedless raisins

a baking tray lined with nonstick parchment paper

Makes about 20

Perfect to serve with after dinner coffee, these chocolate disks are decorated with raisins and chunks of praline.

Put the chocolate into a heatproof bowl set over a saucepan of steaming but not boiling water and melt gently (do not let the base of the bowl touch the water). Let cool for 2 minutes. Drop 1 teaspoon of the chocolate onto a baking tray lined with nonstick parchment paper, then spread it to a disk, about 3½ inches diameter. Press 2 hazelnut-size pieces of praline and 2 raisins into the chocolate. Repeat using the remaining chocolate, praline, and raisins. Let set in a cool place or the refrigerator, then peel off the paper. Store in an airtight container. Best eaten within 1 week.

chocolate salami

5½ oz. bittersweet chocolate

½ cup heavy cream

½ recipe praline (page 30)

2 oz. candied fruit, finely chopped

nonstick parchment paper

Makes about 20

A mixture of chocolate, praline, and candied fruits is shaped into a sausage, then thinly sliced to resemble a salami—popular in Italy around Christmas.

Put the chocolate into a bowl. Put the cream into a saucepan, heat until hot, then pour over the chocolate. Stir the praline and candied fruit into the chocolate mixture. Spoon onto the parchment paper, then shape into a sausage, about 1¾ inches thick. Wrap up in the paper and chill until firm. Remove the paper, cut into thin slices, and serve.

ginger chocolates

3 oz. bittersweet chocolate, melted

3 oz. crystallized ginger (about 20 pieces)

bamboo skewers

a baking tray lined with nonstick parchment paper

Makes about 20

My editor has a will of iron—she can pass by a box of chocolates without a qualm—but offer her a ginger chocolate and she becomes as incoherent as most chocoholics.

Melt the chocolate as described on page 11. Spear each piece of ginger with a bamboo skewer, then dip the ginger halfway into the chocolate. Alternatively, follow the method in Step 1, page 14 to cover the ginger completely.

tiny florentines

At holiday time, look out for crystallized fruits to replace golden raisins in the mixture. When cold, the flat side of each Florentine is coated with plain or white chocolate, then combed to give a wavy pattern or feathered (dragged) design.

6 tablespoons unsalted butter

3½ tablespoons corn syrup or golden syrup

3 tablespoons all-purpose flour

scant ½ cup chopped almonds

3 tablespoons chopped dried candied citrus peel

scant ½ cup golden raisins or candied fruits

½ cup candied cherries, chopped

4 oz. chocolate—bittersweet, or white—or some of each, melted

2 baking trays lined with nonstick parchment paper

Makes about 20

Put the butter and syrup into a heavy saucepan and heat until melted. Stir in all the remaining ingredients except the chocolate.

Put teaspoons of the mixture onto the prepared baking trays, spacing them well apart. Flatten lightly, then bake in a preheated oven at 350°F for 7–8 minutes until light golden brown. Remove from the oven and let cool for 1–2 minutes or until firm enough to transfer to a wire rack to cool completely.

When cool, coat the flat underside of each Florentine with melted chocolate and, using a serrated frosting spatula or fork, make a wavy pattern in the chocolate. Let set, chocolate side up. Store in a cool place in an airtight container.

Best eaten within 1 week.

chocolate truffles

This basic recipe is sublime, but you can also add liqueur to the mixture.

³/₄ cup plus 2 tablespoons heavy cream

10¹/₂ oz. bittersweet chocolate, finely chopped

To coat

9¹/₂ oz. bittersweet or white chocolate, melted

a heaping ¹/₂ cup finest-quality cocoa powder, sifted

a pastry bag fitted with a ¹/₂-inch plain tip (optional)

several baking trays lined with nonstick parchment paper or wax paper

Makes 50

1 Put the cream into a saucepan and heat gently until boiling. Remove from the heat and let cool for several minutes.

Put the chopped chocolate into a heatproof bowl, then pour over the hot cream.* Set aside for several minutes.

*Note If you wish to add alcohol, do so before adding the cream. Suitable choices include 3 tablespoons Drambuie, dark rum, Cognac, Tia Maria, or orange liqueur.

2 Stir gently until just smooth—do not over-mix at this stage. Let cool.

When the mixture is cool but not set, beat vigorously with a wooden spoon until very thick and much lighter in color and texture.

3 Spoon the mixture into a pastry bag fitted with a ½-inch plain tip.

4 Pipe marble-size pieces of the mixture onto the prepared baking trays. Chill until very firm.

Alternatively, you can also use a teaspoon, or roll the mixture into balls with your hands. Chill until very firm.

5 When you are ready to finish the truffles, put the chopped chocolate into a dry heatproof bowl and set over a saucepan of steaming but not boiling water. The water should not touch the base of the bowl or start to boil (page 11). If you like, the chocolate may also be tempered (page 12).

Remove the bowl from the heat.

6 Using 2 forks, briefly dip each truffle into the chocolate until coated.

Return the coated truffles to the lined trays and leave until the coating chocolate is almost set (if the truffles are very cold, this will be immediate).

7 While the coating chocolate is still soft, roll the truffles in cocoa powder. Store in an airtight container in a cool place or the refrigerator until ready to serve.

These eggs made of chocolate and praline (a crunchy mixture of brittle caramel and toasted nuts) can be found in good chocolate stores in France and Italy around Easter. After the filled eggs have set, the shells can be decorated using edible colors, then arranged in an egg carton or basket.

surprise eggs

6 very fresh eggs, with pretty shells

5½ oz. bittersweet chocolate, finely chopped

½ cup minus 1 tablespoon heavy cream

Praline*

⅓ cup whole unblanched almonds

⅓ cup whole skinned hazelnuts

½ cup sugar

a baking tray, well-oiled

Makes 6

Using the tip of a small, sharp knife, gently cut a small hole in the pointed end of each egg, then carefully snip away the shell with shears to cut off the top, leaving a hole about ¾ inch diameter. Empty out the eggs by shaking them over a bowl—the contents can be saved for omelets or scrambled eggs. Wash the empty shells thoroughly, then set them on a piece of wax paper in a baking dish and dry them in a preheated oven at 300°F for about 15 minutes. Let cool.

Meanwhile, to make the praline, put the nuts and sugar into a small, heavy saucepan and heat gently on top of the stove. Stir frequently with a wooden spoon until the sugar melts, then watch it carefully, stirring frequently, as it cooks and turns chestnut brown, and the nuts start to pop. Take care with hot caramel, because splashes can burn you.

Lift the saucepan off the heat, quickly pour the mixture onto the oiled baking tray and, using a wooden spoon, spread it out evenly. Leave until completely cold and set, then coarsely break up the praline with a rolling pin or grind it in a food processor.

Put the chopped chocolate into a heatproof bowl. Put the cream into a heavy saucepan, heat until hot but not boiling, then pour it over the chocolate. Leave for 1 minute, then stir gently. Let cool for 5–10 minutes until thick, then stir in the praline. Stand the egg shells upright in an egg carton or rack and carefully spoon the chocolate mixture into the shells. Chill overnight until firm, then remove from the refrigerator 2 hours before serving.

*Note Use this praline recipe to make the Chocolate Dials and Chocolate Salami on page 23.

baking

No scent has ever been invented that rivals the aroma of chocolate baking: it fills the whole house so everyone knows just what lies in store for them. Here's a fabulous array of cakes, cookies, muffins, brownies, even doughnuts—from fast and simple to simply luxurious.

A favorite with many generations of cake-lovers, this simple creamed sponge is the basis of scores of recipes, from cupcakes to richly frosted gâteaux and hot desserts. For the best results, use extra large eggs and unsalted butter, all at room temperature. An electric mixer is a good investment if you like making cakes—it gives the mixture a much lighter texture, as well as saving time and arm power. The sponges can be sandwiched and topped with a variety of fillings and frostings (pages 38–39), such as the ganache shown here, or with whipped cream or dark cherry jam.

classic chocolate sponge cake

1½ sticks unsalted butter, at room temperature

¾ cup plus 2 tablespoons sugar

3 extra large eggs, at room temperature

1 teaspoon vanilla extract

1 cup self-rising flour

⅓ cup unsweetened cocoa powder

2 tablespoons milk

2 cake pans, 8 inches diameter, buttered and bottoms lined with parchment paper

Serves 8

Put the butter into a mixing bowl and, using a wooden spoon or electric mixer, beat until creamy. Beat in the sugar and continue beating until the mixture is very light and fluffy.

Break the eggs into a glass measuring cup or bowl, add the vanilla extract, and beat with a fork until slightly frothy. Gradually beat the eggs into the butter and sugar mixture, beating well after each addition. Sift the flour and cocoa onto the mixture, add the milk, then, using a large metal spoon, gently fold into the creamed mixture. As soon as the mixture is thoroughly blended, with no visible streaks, divide it equally between the 2 prepared pans and spread evenly.

Bake in a preheated oven at 350°F for 15–20 minutes or until the sponge springs back when gently pressed in the center, is starting to color on top, and has shrunk away from the sides of the pan. Invert onto a wire rack and let cool completely before filling and frosting.

Store in an airtight container in a cool place. Best eaten within 48 hours.

classic chocolate sponge cake variations

cupcakes

¾ cup whole milk

2½ oz. bittersweet chocolate, finely chopped

scant ⅔ cup sugar

4 tablespoons unsalted butter, at room temperature

½ teaspoon vanilla extract

1 large egg, beaten

1½ cups self-rising flour

2 tablespoons chocolate chips or chopped plain chocolate

fudge frosting (page 39), (optional)

a 12-cup muffin pan, lined with paper muffin cups

Makes 12

Put the milk into a saucepan and heat until just scalding. Put the chocolate and one-third of the sugar into a bowl, pour over the milk, and stir until smooth. Let cool. Put the butter into a bowl, then add the remaining sugar and vanilla. Using a wooden spoon, beat until light and fluffy, then gradually beat in the egg. Stir in the chocolate mixture alternately with the flour. Stir in the chips. Spoon into the muffin cups until three-quarters full. Bake in a preheated oven at 350°F for 15–18 minutes until the cakes spring back when pressed in the center. Let cool, then add fudge topping, if using.

fairy cakes

1½ sticks unsalted butter, at room temperature

¾ cup plus 2 tablespoons sugar

3 extra large eggs, at room temperature

1 teaspoon vanilla extract

1 cup self-rising flour

⅓ cup unsweetened cocoa powder

2 tablespoons milk

chocolate frostings (pages 38–39), (optional)

several 12-cup muffin pans, lined with paper muffin cups

Makes 24

Put all the ingredients into a mixing bowl and, using a wooden spoon or electric mixer, mix until thoroughly blended—if using an electric mixer, use medium speed. Spoon about 1 tablespoon of the mixture into each muffin cup, until half full. Bake in a preheated oven at 350°F for 12–15 minutes until the sponge springs back when gently pressed in the center. Let cool on a wire rack. Serve plain or decorate with a chocolate topping of your choice.

gâteau arabica

2 sticks unsalted butter, at room temperature

1½ cups firmly packed light brown sugar

4 extra large eggs, beaten

¾ cup all-purpose flour

1⅓ cups unsweetened cocoa powder

2 teaspoons baking powder

¼ cup espresso coffee, cooled to room temperature

arabica frosting (page 39)

2 cake pans, 8 inches diameter, buttered, lined with parchment paper

Serves 8

Put the butter into a bowl and, using a wooden spoon or electric mixer, beat until creamy. Beat in the sugar and continue beating until the mixture is light and fluffy. Break the eggs into a separate bowl and beat with a fork until slightly frothy. Gradually beat the eggs into the mixture, beating well after each addition. Sift the flour, cocoa, and baking powder onto the mixture. Add the cool coffee and gently fold into the creamed mixture until blended. Spoon into the prepared pans and bake in a preheated oven at 350°F for 25–30 minutes until the sponge springs back when gently pressed in the center. Invert onto a wire rack, remove the parchment paper, and let cool completely before sandwiching and topping with arabica frosting.

speckled sponge

1½ sticks unsalted butter, at room temperature

¾ cup plus 2 tablespoons sugar

3 extra large eggs, at room temperature

1 teaspoon vanilla extract

1⅓ cups self-rising flour

2 tablespoons milk

2 oz. bittersweet chocolate, finely chopped, or chocolate chips

chocolate frosting (pages 38–39)

2 cake pans, 8 inches diameter, buttered, lined with parchment paper

Serves 8

Put the butter into a bowl and, using a wooden spoon or electric mixer, beat until creamy. Beat in the sugar and continue beating until light and fluffy. Break the eggs into a separate bowl, add the vanilla extract and beat with a fork until slightly frothy. Gradually beat the eggs into the mixture, beating well after each addition. Sift the flour onto the mixture, add the milk, and gently fold in until thoroughly blended. Stir in the chocolate. Spoon into the pans and bake in a preheated oven at 350°F for 25–30 minutes until the sponge springs back when gently pressed in the center. Invert onto a wire rack, remove the parchment paper, and let cool. Layer and top with your chosen frosting.

fillings and frostings

light fluffy butter frosting

Not too rich – an ideal frosting for children's party cakes.

1 stick plus 1 tablespoon unsalted butter, at room temperature

3 cups confectioners' sugar, sifted

3 tablespoons unsweetened cocoa powder, sifted

3–4 tablespoons milk

**Makes enough to fill and top
1 sponge cake or top 24 cupcakes**

Put the butter into a bowl and, using a wooden spoon or electric mixer, beat until very soft and creamy. Gradually beat in the confectioners' sugar, cocoa, and milk to make a thick, smooth frosting: if using an electric mixer, use low speed.

Variations To make a mocha frosting, replace the milk with cold coffee. To make a white vanilla frosting, omit the cocoa and beat in 1 teaspoon vanilla extract.

sour cream filling and frosting

Rich, silky-smooth, and velvety.

6 oz. good-quality milk chocolate, finely chopped

3½ oz. bittersweet chocolate, finely chopped

1 cup sour cream

**Makes enough to fill and top
1 sponge cake**

Put both chocolates into a heatproof bowl set over a saucepan of steaming but not boiling water and melt gently (do not let the base of the bowl touch the water). Remove from the heat and stir gently until smooth. Using electric beaters, beat in the cream. The mixture will become thick and glossy. In cool conditions, the mixture will be spreadable immediately. In warm weather, chill for a few minutes until thick enough to spread. If the mixture becomes too hard, soften by setting the bowl briefly over a saucepan of steaming water.

extra rich and creamy frosting

Cream cheese gives a richer, heavier frosting.

1 stick plus 1 tablespoon unsalted butter, at room temperature

4½ oz. cream cheese, about ½ cup

1 teaspoon vanilla extract

3½ cups confectioners' sugar, sifted

¼ cup unsweetened cocoa powder, sifted

**Makes enough to fill and top
1 sponge cake**

Put the butter, cream cheese, and vanilla into a mixing bowl and, using a wooden spoon or electric mixer, beat until soft and creamy. Gradually beat in the confectioners' sugar and cocoa to make a thick, smooth mixture: if using an electric mixer use low speed.

arabica filling and frosting

A French-style buttercream enriched with egg yolks. Add coffee to taste for a mild or more intense flavor. Decorate the finished cake with chocolate coffee beans for extra verve.

1½ sticks unsalted butter, at room temperature

1⅓ cups confectioners' sugar, sifted

2 large egg yolks

3 tablespoons espresso coffee or 3 teaspoons instant coffee dissolved in 3 tablespoons hot water (or to taste), then cooled to room temperature

Makes enough to fill and top
1 sponge cake

Put all the ingredients into a mixing bowl and, using a wooden spoon or electric mixer, beat until smooth, thick, and creamy: if using an electric mixer use low speed.

fudge frosting

A rich, very chocolaty topping for large cakes, loaf cakes, and cupcakes.

3½ oz. bittersweet chocolate, finely chopped

1 tablespoon corn syrup or golden syrup

2 tablespoons unsalted butter, at room temperature

Makes enough to fill and top
1 sponge cake or top 12 cupcakes

Put the chocolate into a heatproof bowl set over a saucepan of steaming water but not boiling water and melt gently (do not let the base of the bowl touch the water). Remove from the heat and stir in the corn syrup and butter. When smooth, let cool, stirring occasionally, until thick and on the point of setting. If the mixture sets before you are ready to use it, gently melt over very low heat. Spread over the finished cake and let set.

ganache

The smoothest and most bitter chocolate frosting is made from equal quantities of chocolate and heavy cream. For a softer frosting, use a little more cream than chocolate; for an darker but harder covering, use a little more chocolate than cream.

scant ½ cup heavy cream

4 oz. bittersweet chocolate, finely chopped

Makes enough to fill and top
1 sponge cake

Put the cream into a saucepan and heat until scalding hot. Put the chocolate into a heatproof bowl, then pour over the hot cream. Leave for about 2 minutes, then stir until just smooth. Let cool until thick enough to spread.

This traditional German recipe is nothing like the commercial cakes on sale these days. This is the real thing (and note that the sponge contains no flour).

black forest gâteau

Chocolate sponge

9 extra large eggs, separated

1 cup sugar

1 cup unsweetened cocoa powder, sifted

Cherry filling

25 oz. can Morello cherries in kirsch syrup—or syrup plus 3 tablespoons kirsch (a 50 ml miniature)

scant 2 cups heavy cream

3 tablespoons sugar

2 oz. bittersweet chocolate, grated

3 cake pans, 8 inches diameter, buttered and bottoms lined with parchment paper

Serves 8–10

To make the sponge cakes, put the egg yolks and sugar into a bowl and, using electric beaters or electric mixer, beat until very thick and mousse-like—when the beaters are lifted, a wide ribbon-like trail slowly falls back into the bowl. Sift the cocoa onto the mixture and gently fold in with a large metal spoon.

Put the egg whites into a spotlessly clean, greasefree bowl and beat, using an electric mixer, electric beaters, or rotary beaters, until stiff peaks form. Carefully fold into the yolk mixture in 3 batches. Divide the mixture between the 3 prepared pans, then bake in a preheated oven at 350°F for 20–25 minutes until the cakes spring back when gently pressed, and have shrunk away from the sides of the pans. Let cool in the pans before inverting onto a wire rack and peeling off the parchment paper.

Drain the cherries in a strainer and save the syrup: you will need 7 tablespoons (if using cherries in sugar syrup, put ¼ cup of the sugar syrup into a bowl and add the 3 tablespoons kirsch). When the cherries have been well drained, leave them on paper towels. Reserve 12 to decorate.

Set one of the cooled sponges onto a pretty serving plate, then sprinkle 2 tablespoons of the kirsch syrup over the sponge.

Put the cream into a bowl and, using an electric mixer or beaters, whip the cream until soft peaks form. Sprinkle the sugar over the cream and whip until slightly thicker. Set aside half the cream to cover the cake. Spread half the remaining cream onto the bottom layer of sponge. Press half the cherries into the cream. Sprinkle the second sponge layer with the kirsch syrup as before, then gently set on top of the first layer. Spread with cream and press in the cherries as before. Top with the final layer of sponge. Sprinkle with the remaining kirsch syrup. Cover the top and sides of the cake with the rest of the cream— you can either spread or pipe the cream—then decorate with the reserved cherries and grated chocolate. Chill until ready to serve. Best eaten within 48 hours.

My editor, Elsa Petersen-Schepelern, and her sister Kirsten are both great cooks, and Kirsten's chocolate cake is legendary— a fabulous combination of moist dark sponge, thick nutty filling, and dark chocolate frosting. An electric mixer will really help here.

chocolate layer cake

heaping 1/2 cup unsweetened cocoa powder

2 cups self-rising flour

1/4 teaspoon salt

1/2 teaspoon baking powder

1 stick plus 1 tablespoon unsalted butter, at room temperature

1 cup sugar

3 extra large eggs, beaten

1 teaspoon vanilla extract

1 cup less 1 tablespoon milk

Nutty filling

1 cup pure maple syrup

2 extra large egg whites

1/4 cup chopped pecans

Frosting

3 tablespoons unsweetened cocoa powder

1 tablespoon butter, at room temperature

1 tablespoon maple syrup

1 extra large egg white

1 1/2 cups confectioners' sugar, sifted

3 cake pans, 8 inches diameter, buttered and bottoms lined with parchment paper

Serves 12

Sift the cocoa into a heatproof bowl, then stir in 1/2 cup boiling water to make a smooth paste. Let cool.

Sift the flour, salt, and baking powder 3 times onto a sheet of wax paper.

Put the butter into a bowl and, using a wooden spoon or an electric mixer, beat until creamy. Beat in the sugar thoroughly, until the mixture is light and fluffy. Gradually beat in the eggs and vanilla, then gradually beat in the cooled cocoa mixture. Using a large metal spoon, fold in the flour mixture alternately with the milk. When thoroughly combined, divide the mixture evenly between the 3 pans and spread evenly. Bake in a preheated oven at 375°F for about 20 minutes, until just firm to the touch. Invert onto a wire rack and let cool.

To make the filling, put the maple syrup into a heavy saucepan and bring to a boil until it reaches 238°F on a candy thermometer (soft ball stage). This will take about 5 minutes: take care as the syrup can bubble up alarmingly if the heat is too high. While the syrup is heating, put the egg whites into a clean, greasefree bowl and beat until stiff peaks form. When the syrup has reached the correct stage, pour it onto the egg whites in a thin steady stream, beating constantly. Continue beating until the mixture is very thick and fluffy. Stir in the chopped nuts, then use to layer and coat the cakes.

To make the frosting, sift the cocoa into a heatproof bowl, add the butter and maple syrup, then stir in 1/2 cup boiling water to make a thick, smooth paste. Add the unbeaten egg white, then, using a wooden spoon or electric mixer, gradually beat in the confectioners' sugar to make a thin, smooth, spreadable frosting. Pour the frosting over the cake and gently spread it so it covers the entire cake. Chill for a few minutes until firm, then serve at room temperature.

sachertorte

The most famous of all the Viennese cakes, this sumptuous chocolate cake was invented in 1832 by the chef at the Hotel Sacher. At the hotel, you can still buy a sachertorte, made from the original recipe and packaged in a stylish wooden box.

7 oz. bittersweet chocolate, finely chopped

1 stick plus 4 tablespoons unsalted butter, at room temperature

³/₄ cup sugar

5 extra large eggs, plus 1 egg white

1 cup all-purpose flour

½ teaspoon baking powder

Apricot glaze

¹/₄ cup apricot preserves

1 teaspoon lemon juice

Chocolate frosting

½ cup heavy cream

7 oz. bittersweet chocolate, chopped

a little melted milk chocolate, to pipe (optional)

whipped cream, to serve

a springform or false-bottom cake pan, 9 inches diameter, buttered and bottom lined with parchment paper

a wax paper pastry bag (optional)

Serves 12

1 Put the chocolate into a heatproof bowl set over a saucepan of steaming but not boiling water and melt gently (do not let the base of the bowl touch the water). Remove from the heat and let cool.

2 Put the butter into a large bowl and, using a wooden spoon or electric beaters, beat until creamy. Add half the sugar and beat until light and fluffy.

3 Separate the eggs. Put the 6 whites into a large, spotlessly clean and greasefree bowl.

Using electric beaters or mixer, beat 5 of the yolks into the creamed mixture, one at a time, beating well after each addition. (Reserve the remaining yolk for another purpose.)

4 Stir in the cooled chocolate.

5 Sift the flour and baking powder onto the mixture and fold in gently with a large metal spoon.

6 Using an electric mixer or rotary beaters, beat the egg whites until stiff peaks form, then beat in the remaining sugar, 1 tablespoon at a time.

7 Fold into the chocolate mixture in 3 batches.

8 When the mixture is evenly blended, spoon into the prepared pan and level the surface. Bake in a preheated oven at 325°F for 1 hour or until a skewer inserted in the center comes out clean. Let cool in the pan for 10 minutes, then carefully invert onto a wire rack, remove the parchment paper, and let cool completely. (The flat base will be easier to frost.)

9 To make the glaze, put the apricot preserves, lemon juice, and 1 tablespoon water into a small saucepan, heat gently, then bring gently to a boil, stirring constantly. Remove from the heat and push through a strainer into a bowl.

10 Brush the hot glaze over the top and sides of the cake (the cake can also be split in half horizontally and sandwiched with extra glaze). Let cool on the wire rack.

11 Meanwhile, to make the frosting, put the cream into a small saucepan and heat until almost boiling. Put the chopped chocolate into a heatproof bowl and pour in the hot cream.

12 Leave for 2 minutes, then stir until the frosting is smooth and glossy.

13 Put a plate under the wire rack to catch the drips, then pour the frosting over the cake so it covers the top and sides—if necessary, spread the frosting to cover any bare patches. Let set in a cool place, but not the refrigerator.

14 If liked, put some melted chocolate into a wax paper pastry bag and pipe the word "Sacher" or the letter "S" on top of the cake.

Cut into small slices and serve with whipped cream. For best results, use a sharp knife and, before making each cut, dip the knife into hot water and wipe it dry. Store the cake in an airtight container in a cool place.

Best eaten within 1 week. The unfrosted cake can be frozen for up to 1 month.

black and white chocolate marble loaf cake

The classic pound cake recipe (known as *quatre quatre* in France and *sandkuchen* in Germany), uses equal weights of butter, flour, sugar, and eggs. It's very easy to turn the basic sponge mixture into an impressive, richly flavored marbled loaf. Serve thick slices with a cup of tea or coffee. The cake is also perfect for picnics, but for a real treat, serve warm for dessert with plenty of whipped cream, custard, or even Rich Dark Chocolate Sauce (page 106).

2 sticks unsalted butter, at room temperature

2 cups plus 2 tablespoons sugar

4 extra large eggs, at room temperature, lightly beaten

1 teaspoon vanilla extract

1⅔ cups self-rising flour

3 oz. bittersweet chocolate, chopped

1 tablespoon unsweetened cocoa powder

3 oz. white chocolate, chopped

a loaf pan, 2 lb., buttered and bottom lined with parchment paper

Makes 1 large loaf

Put the butter into a large mixing bowl and, using a wooden spoon or electric mixer, beat until very creamy. Beat in the sugar and continue beating for about 2 minutes until the mixture is lighter in color and consistency. Gradually beat in the eggs, then beat in the vanilla extract. Sift the flour onto the creamed mixture and gently fold in with a large metal spoon.

Spoon half the cake mixture into another mixing bowl. Put the plain chocolate into a heatproof bowl set over a saucepan of steaming but not boiling water and melt gently (do not let the base of the bowl touch the water). Remove the bowl from the heat and let cool. Sift the cocoa onto one portion of cake mixture, add the cooled melted plain chocolate, then, using a large metal spoon, carefully fold in until evenly mixed.

Put the white chocolate into a heatproof bowl set over a saucepan of steaming but not boiling water and melt gently (do not let the base of the bowl touch the water). Remove the bowl from the heat and let cool. Using a clean metal spoon, fold into the remaining portion of cake mixture.

Spoon both cake mixtures into the prepared pan, using each mixture alternately. To make the marbling, draw a knife through the mixtures and swirl together.

Bake in a preheated oven at 350°F for about 1¼ hours or until a skewer inserted in the center comes out clean. Invert gently onto a wire rack, remove the parchment paper, and let cool completely.

Store in an airtight container. Best eaten within 5 days. The cake can be frozen for up to 1 month.

pain d'épices au chocolat

The classic French *pain d'épices*—honey spice cake—should be made with equal weights of flour and honey, and flavored with *quatre épices*, a ready-made mixture of spices usually available only in French gourmet stores.* The grated chocolate is a fairly new addition to the medieval recipe and replaces the traditional chopped almonds and candied peel. Try this cake, thickly sliced, with a cup of good coffee.

1½ cups all-purpose flour

¾ cup rye flour

¼ teaspoon salt

2 teaspoons baking powder

½ teaspoon ground cinnamon

½ teaspoon ground cloves

½ teaspoon quatre épices*

3½ oz. bittersweet chocolate, grated or finely chopped

¾ cup plus 2 tablespoons clear honey

2 large egg yolks

5 tablespoons milk

Chocolate glaze

2 oz. bittersweet chocolate, chopped

2 tablespoons sugar

3 tablespoons milk

a loaf pan, 1 lb,, buttered and bottom lined with parchment paper

Makes 1 medium loaf

Sift both the flours, salt, baking powder, and all the spices into a mixing bowl. Stir in the grated chocolate. Add the honey, egg yolks, and milk and mix with a wooden spoon to make a thick, heavy cake mixture. Spoon into the prepared pan and level the surface. Bake immediately in a preheated oven at 350°F for about 45 minutes until the loaf turns golden brown and a skewer inserted in the center comes out clean. Invert onto a wire rack, remove the parchment paper, and let cool.

As soon as the loaf is out of the oven, make the glaze. Put the chocolate, sugar, and milk into a small, heavy saucepan and heat gently, stirring, until the chocolate has melted. Bring to a boil, still stirring, let bubble for about 5 seconds, then remove from the heat. Pour, spoon, or brush the hot, thin glaze over the warm loaf and let it drip down the sides. Leave the loaf until completely cool before slicing. Store in an airtight container.

Best eaten within 5 days. The unglazed loaf can be frozen for up to 1 month.

*Note To make *quatre épices*, the late Jane Grigson suggested mixing 7 parts finely ground black pepper with 1 part each of ground cloves, ground ginger, and grated nutmeg. Store in a screw-top bottle.

As with the perfect brownie recipe, finding the ultimate devil's food cake involved years of tasting. Once again, my mother-in-law in Maine came up with a lovely recipe—a sponge with a very light texture, properly dark in color, and with great flavor.

devil's food cake

4 oz. bittersweet chocolate, finely chopped

½ cup sour cream

1 cup firmly packed light brown sugar

2 cups all-purpose flour

a good pinch of salt

3 tablespoons unsweetened cocoa powder

1 teaspoon baking soda

1 stick unsalted butter, at room temperature

1 cup sugar

2 very large eggs, separated

1 teaspoon vanilla extract

¾ cup water, at room temperature

Frosting and filling

5 oz. bittersweet chocolate, finely chopped

5 oz. milk chocolate, finely chopped

1 cup sour cream

3 cake pans, 8 inches diameter, or 2 cake pans, 9 inches diameter, buttered and bottoms lined with parchment paper

Serves 10–12

Put the chopped chocolate, sour cream, and brown sugar into a heavy saucepan and set over very low heat. Stir occasionally until melted and smooth but don't let the mixture become hot. Remove from the heat and set aside until needed.

Sift the flour with the salt, cocoa, and baking soda onto a sheet of wax paper and set aside.

Put the butter into a bowl and, using a wooden spoon or electric beaters, beat until creamy. Gradually beat in the sugar. Beat well, then beat in the egg yolks one at a time, followed by the vanilla extract. Mix in the flour mixture, 1 tablespoon at a time, alternately with the water (if using the mixer, use low speed and mix as little as possible). When thoroughly blended, work in the melted chocolate mixture. Spoon the mixture into the prepared pans, to fill evenly, then bake in a preheated oven at 350°F for 25 minutes for the smaller cakes or 30 minutes for the larger ones. The cakes are cooked when they spring back when gently pressed in the center and have slightly shrunk away from the sides of the pans. Let cool for 5 minutes, then invert onto a wire rack, remove the parchment paper, and cool completely.

To make the frosting and filling, put the bittersweet and milk chocolates into a heatproof bowl set over a saucepan of steaming but not boiling water and leave until melted (do not let the base of the bowl touch the water). Remove the bowl from the heat, stir gently until smooth, then beat in the cream. Leave until very thick and spreadable (in hot weather you may need to chill it briefly).

Set one cake aside and spread frosting on top of the remaining cake(s). Sandwich the layers together, with the plain one on top. Spread the top and sides of the cake with frosting. (In hot weather, chill the cake for a few minutes until the frosting is firm.) Keep in a cool place until ready to serve.

The unfrosted cake may be stored in an airtight container for up to 24 hours. The finished cake is best eaten within 5 days. The unfrosted cakes can be frozen for up to 1 month.

Cut into this chocolate-covered cake and you will find a rich, tangy orange sponge interior. Serve with afternoon coffee or as a dessert with piles of whipped cream or scoops of vanilla or chocolate ice cream (page 110).

surprise cake

1½ sticks unsalted butter, at room temperature

¾ cup plus 2 tablespoons sugar

grated zest of 2 unwaxed oranges

3 extra large eggs, beaten

1¼ cups self-rising flour, sifted

2 tablespoons fresh orange juice (from about ½ orange)

Orange syrup

½ cup freshly squeezed orange juice (from about 1½ oranges)

1–2 tablespoons orange liqueur, such as Cointreau or Grand Marnier (optional)

⅓ cup plus 1 tablespoon sugar

Chocolate frosting

5½ oz. chocolate, finely chopped

4 tablespoons unsalted butter, cut into small pieces

a springform or deep cake pan, 8 inches diameter, buttered and bottom lined with parchment paper

Serves 8

Put the butter into a mixing bowl and, using a wooden spoon or electric mixer, beat until creamy. Add the sugar and the orange zest and beat until light and fluffy. Gradually beat in the eggs, beating well after each addition. Using a large metal spoon, fold in the flour in 3 batches, adding the orange juice with the last batch of flour. Spoon the batter into the prepared pan and level the surface. Bake in a preheated oven at 350°F for 35–40 minutes.

While the cake is baking, make the orange syrup. Put the orange juice (if using liqueur, replace 1–2 tablespoons of the orange juice with liqueur) and sugar into a bowl and, using a large metal spoon, mix until the sugar dissolves.

As soon as the cake is well risen, golden brown, and a skewer inserted in the center comes out clean, remove from the oven and transfer to a wire rack (do not take it out of the pan). Prick the cake all over with a skewer or toothpick and slowly spoon the orange syrup over the cake, until it has all been absorbed. Leave until cold before removing from the pan.

To make the frosting, put the chocolate and butter into a heatproof bowl set over a saucepan of steaming but not boiling water and melt gently (do not let the base of the bowl touch the water). Remove the bowl from the heat, gently stir the chocolate until smooth, then spread it evenly over the top and sides of the cake. Let set, then transfer to a serving plate. Store in an airtight container.

Best eaten within 6 days. The cooled cake, minus the syrup, can be frozen for up to 1 month. Defrost the cake, then gently warm the syrup, pour over the cake, and finish as in the main recipe.

It's a shame to keep fruit cakes just for Christmas and weddings. This one is simple, fairly light, and easy to make for a weekend party. With a combination of almond sponge, glacé cherries (the naturally colored ones are best), the largest and juiciest raisins you can find, walnut halves, and chunks of plain chocolate, there's no need for a frosting.

chocolate fruit and nut cake

1 cup large seedless raisins

½ cup candied cherries, halved

2 tablespoons rum, orange juice, or cold black tea

2 sticks unsalted butter, at room temperature

1 cup plus 2 tablespoons sugar

4 extra large eggs, at room temperature, beaten

1⅔ cups all-purpose flour

1 tablespoon baking powder

a pinch of salt

1 cup ground almonds

3½ oz. bittersweet chocolate, coarsely chopped

1 cup walnut pieces

a springform or deep cake pan, 9 inches diameter, bottom lined with parchment paper

Serves 10

Put the raisins, cherries, and rum into a small bowl, stir, then cover with plastic wrap and let soak for at least 2 hours, preferably overnight.

Put the butter into a mixing bowl and, using a wooden spoon or electric mixer, beat until creamy. Add the sugar and beat until light and fluffy. Gradually beat in the eggs. Sift the flour, baking powder, salt, and ground almonds onto the creamed mixture, and using a large metal spoon, fold the dry ingredients into the mixture. Add the fruit and rum mixture, the chopped chocolate, and walnuts and gently stir in until thoroughly blended. Spoon the mixture into the prepared pan and level the surface.

Bake in a preheated oven at 350°F for 1–1¼ hours until the top is golden brown, firm to the touch, and a skewer inserted into the center comes out clean. Let cool in the pan, then invert onto a wire rack, remove the parchment paper, and cool completely. Wrap in wax paper and keep overnight before cutting. Store in an airtight container.

Best eaten within 1 week. It can be frozen for up to 1 month.

This is what I make when we need a treat—warm, slightly soft brownies packed with nuts, topped with a few shavings of white chocolate or a scoop of vanilla ice cream, and lots of hot, very chocolaty fudge sauce. The combination of the contrasting textures, temperatures, and tastes is truly sublime.

fudge brownies with chocolate fudge sauce

3½ oz. bittersweet chocolate, finely chopped

1 stick plus 1 tablespoon unsalted butter, at room temperature

1⅓ cups sugar

1 teaspoon vanilla extract

2 extra large eggs, beaten

scant ¾ cup all-purpose flour

2 tablespoons unsweetened cocoa powder

a pinch of salt

1 cup pecan halves or walnut pieces

Chocolate fudge sauce

7 oz. bittersweet chocolate, finely chopped

4 tablespoons unsalted butter

2 tablespoons sugar

2 tablespoons corn syrup or golden syrup

¾ cup milk or light cream

*a cake pan, 8 inches square, buttered and bottom lined with parchment paper**

Makes 16

Put the chocolate into a heatproof bowl set over a saucepan of steaming but not boiling water and melt gently (do not let the base of the bowl touch the water). Remove the bowl from the heat and let cool while making the mixture.

Put the butter into a large mixing bowl and, using a wooden spoon or electric mixer, beat until soft and creamy. Add the sugar and vanilla extract and continue beating until the mixture is soft and fluffy. Gradually beat in the eggs.

Sift the flour, cocoa, and salt onto the mixture, then spoon the melted chocolate on top and gently stir together until thoroughly mixed. Stir in the nuts. Spoon the mixture into the prepared pan and level the surface.

Bake in a preheated oven at 350°F for 30–35 minutes until a skewer inserted halfway between the sides of the pan and the center comes out clean—it is important that the center is just set but still slightly soft and not cake-like. Let cool in the pan, then remove from the pan* and cut into 16 squares. Eat warm or at room temperature with the chocolate sauce. When cold, the brownies may be stored in an airtight container.

To make the chocolate sauce, put all the ingredients into a small, heavy saucepan and set over low heat. Stir gently until melted and smooth. Continue heating and stirring until the mixture is almost at boiling point. Remove from the heat and serve immediately. The sauce will thicken as it cools.

The brownies are best eaten within 5 days, or can be frozen for up to 1 month. The chocolate sauce is best eaten the same day or, when cool, cover with plastic wrap and store in the refrigerator for up to 48 hours. Reheat gently.

Note To make removal easier, I cut the parchment paper wider, so it overlaps the edges of the pan. After cooling, remove the uncut slab of brownies using the overlapping paper as handles. Work gently, to avoid cracking the top.

A cross between biscuits and shortcake, these muffins are rich, moist, and very crumbly. Eat warm—there is no need to serve them with butter.

chocolate crumble muffins

1¾ cups self-rising flour

a pinch of salt

⅓ cup plus 1 tablespoon sugar

6 tablespoons unsalted butter, chilled and cut into small pieces

3 oz. bittersweet chocolate, grated or finely chopped

⅓ cup finely chopped unsalted nuts (optional)

2 tablespoons very finely chopped dried candied citrus peel

1 extra large egg

about ¾ cup light cream

chocolate chips or almonds, to decorate

a 12-hole muffin pan, lined with paper muffin cases or well buttered

Makes 12

Sift the flour, salt, and sugar into a mixing bowl. Add the butter and, using the tips of your fingers, rub in until the mixture resembles fine bread crumbs. Stir in the chocolate, nuts, and citrus peel. Break the egg into a glass measuring cup, then add enough cream to make 1 cup. Add the egg mixture to the bowl and mix with a round-bladed knife until the dough comes together—it will be quite sticky.

Divide the dough equally between the prepared muffin cases, then decorate with chocolate chips or almonds.

Bake in a preheated oven at 425°F for 10 minutes, then reduce the heat to 350°F and bake for a further 5–10 minutes or until golden brown and firm to the touch. Remove from the oven and let cool on a wire rack. When completely cold, store in an airtight container.

Best eaten within 2 days. Can be frozen for up to 1 month.

Making doughnuts is something I do on impulse on a gloomy winter's afternoon. I prefer to use a rich, biscuit-like dough rather than a yeast dough, as much for the taste and very light texture as for the instant gratification. The frosting is rich and glossy, but if you prefer sugar-coated doughnuts, roll the hot doughnuts in sugar mixed with a little ground cinnamon. The buttermilk can be replaced with 3 tablespoons plain yogurt made up to 1/2 cup with milk.

chocolate doughnuts

4 tablespoons unsalted butter, very soft

scant 1/3 cup sugar

1 extra large egg, lightly beaten

1/2 cup less 1 tablespoon buttermilk

1 2/3 cups all-purpose flour

1 teaspoon baking powder

1/2 teaspoon baking soda

1/4 cup unsweetened cocoa powder

1/4 teaspoon salt

1 teaspoon ground cinnamon

several gratings of fresh nutmeg

peanut or safflower oil, for frying

Chocolate icing

3 oz. bittersweet chocolate, finely chopped

scant 3/4 cup confectioners' sugar, sifted

2 round cookie cutters, 1 and 3 inches diameter

Makes 8

Put the butter, sugar, egg, and buttermilk into a large mixing bowl. Sift the flour, baking powder, baking soda, cocoa, salt, and spices on top and, using a wooden spoon or electric mixer (on low speed), mix until the ingredients are thoroughly blended. Turn the mixture out onto a floured work surface and knead gently to make a smooth dough—slightly soft but not sticky, rather like a biscuit dough. If necessary work in a little more flour.

Using floured hands, pat out the dough about 1/2 inch thick. Cut out disks using the 3-inch cutter, then stamp out the centers with the smaller cutter. Knead the trimmings together, then use to make more doughnuts.

Fill a large saucepan with frying basket one-third full with the oil (or an electric deep-fryer to the manufacturer's recommended level). Heat the oil to 350°F or until a cube of bread will brown in 40 seconds. Fry the doughnuts 2–3 at a time, turning them frequently until darker brown and cooked through, about 4 minutes. Using a slotted spoon, remove from the oil and drain on paper towels.

While the doughnuts are cooling, make the frosting. Put the chocolate into a heatproof bowl set over a saucepan of steaming but not boiling water and melt gently (do not let the base of the bowl touch the water). Remove the bowl from the heat and stir in the sugar and 1/4 cup hot water to make a smooth, runny frosting. Dip the tops of the doughnuts in the frosting and leave on a wire rack until set.

Best eaten the same day.

crescent moons

1 stick unsalted butter,
at room temperature

2–3 drops almond extract

½ cup confectioners' sugar, sifted

a pinch of salt

scant ¾ cup all-purpose flour, sifted

4 oz. slivered almonds, finely ground in a
food processor

To finish

2 oz. bittersweet chocolate, melted

confectioners' sugar, for sprinkling

several baking trays, buttered

Makes about 24

Put the butter and almond extract into a mixing bowl and, using a wooden spoon or electric mixer, beat until very soft and creamy. Gradually beat in the confectioners' sugar, on slow speed if using an electric mixer, then beat well until very fluffy. Work in the salt, flour, and ground almonds and, if necessary, knead gently to bring the dough together. Wrap in plastic and chill for about 20 minutes until firm.

Take a heaping teaspoon of dough and roll it with your hands into a sausage shape about 3 inches long, then curve it to make a crescent. Repeat with the rest of dough and set the crescents well apart on the prepared baking trays. Bake in a preheated oven at 325°F for 15–18 minutes until just firm, but still pale with just the very edges slightly colored. Remove from the oven and let cool on the trays for about 2 minutes or until firm enough to transfer to a wire rack to cool completely.

When cold, dip one end of each crescent into the melted chocolate, then transfer to nonstick parchment paper. Leave in a cool place until set, then sprinkle the plain end with confectioners' sugar. Store the cookies in an airtight container.

Best eaten within 1 week. Not suitable for freezing.

double chocolate macaroons

3 oz. bittersweet chocolate, chopped

2 large egg whites,
at room temperature

1 cup sugar

4 oz. (1 cup) firmly packed slivered
almonds, finely ground in a food
processor

2–3 drops almond extract

Chocolate filling

4 oz. white chocolate, chopped

½ cup heavy cream

*2 baking trays, lined with
nonstick parchment paper*

Makes 8 pairs

Put the bittersweet chocolate into a heatproof bowl set over a saucepan of steaming but not boiling water and melt gently (do not let the base of the bowl touch the water). Remove the bowl from the heat and stir until smooth. Let cool while making the rest of the mixture. Put the egg whites into a spotlessly clean, greasefree bowl and, using electric beaters or mixer, beat until stiff peaks form. Gradually beat in the sugar to make a thick, glossy meringue. Using a large metal spoon, fold in the ground almonds, almond extract, and chocolate and blend well. Put 1 tablespoon of the mixture onto the prepared baking tray and spread to a 2-inch disk. Repeat with the rest of the mixture, spacing well apart.

Bake in a preheated oven at 300°F for 30 minutes until just firm. Remove from the oven and let cool on the trays for about 2 minutes or until firm enough to transfer to a wire rack to cool completely. When cold, peel the macaroons away from the parchment paper.

To make the filling, put the white chocolate and cream into a small, heavy saucepan and heat very gently, stirring occasionally, until melted and smooth. Remove from the heat, let cool, then, using a wooden spoon, beat until thick and fluffy. Use to sandwich the macaroons together and set aside for at least 1 hour before serving. Store in an airtight container.

Best eaten within 5 days. Not suitable for freezing.

giant double chocolate nut cookies

5 oz. bittersweet chocolate, chopped

7 tablespoons unsalted butter, at room temperature

⅓ cup sugar

½ cup firmly packed dark brown sugar

1 very large egg, beaten

½ teaspoon vanilla extract

1 cup all-purpose flour

a pinch of salt

½ teaspoon baking powder

½ cup chopped pecans or walnuts

3½ oz. bittersweet or white chocolate, chopped into chunks

several baking trays, buttered

Makes 16

Chocolate chip cookies with a difference—double chocolate. The chips are chunks of bittersweet or white chocolate, and the mixture is flavored with melted chocolate.

Put the chopped chocolate into a heatproof bowl set over a saucepan of barely simmering water and melt gently (do not let the base of the bowl touch the water). Remove the bowl from the heat and let cool. Meanwhile, using a wooden spoon or electric mixer, beat the butter until creamy. Add the sugars and beat again until light and fluffy. Gradually beat in the egg and vanilla extract, followed by the melted chocolate. Sift the flour, salt, and baking powder into the bowl and stir. When thoroughly mixed, work in the nuts and chocolate chunks. Put heaping tablespoons of the mixture, spaced well apart, onto the prepared baking trays.

Bake in a preheated oven at 350°F for 12–15 minutes until just firm. Remove from the oven and let cool on the trays for 2 minutes or until firm enough to transfer to a wire rack. Let cool completely, then store in an airtight container.

Best eaten within 1 week. Can be frozen for up to 1 month.

black and white cookies

1 stick unsalted butter, at room temperature

½ cup firmly packed light brown sugar

1 very large egg, beaten

6 tablespoons self-rising flour

½ teaspoon baking powder

a pinch of salt

½ teaspoon vanilla extract

1½ cups rolled oats

6½ oz. bittersweet chocolate, chopped into chunks

several baking trays, buttered

Makes about 24

My all-time favorites. For best results, use coarsely chopped bittersweet chocolate rather than chocolate chips.

Put the butter into a large mixing bowl and, using a wooden spoon or electric mixer, beat until creamy. Add the sugar and beat until light and creamy. Gradually beat in the egg, and beat well after the last addition. Sift the flour, baking powder, and salt into the bowl, add the vanilla extract and oats, and stir in. When thoroughly mixed, stir in the chocolate chunks.

Put heaped teaspoons of the mixture, spaced well apart, onto the prepared baking trays, then bake in a preheated oven at 350°F for 12–15 minutes until golden and just firm. Remove from the oven and let cool on the trays for about 2 minutes or until firm enough to transfer to a wire rack. Let cool completely, then store in an airtight container.

Best eaten within 1 week. Can be frozen for up to 1 month.

Keep a bag of these tiny, buttery buns in the freezer for lazy breakfasts. Warm through and eat with steaming cups of coffee or hot chocolate (page 119). The dough is simpler to make than the traditional recipe, particularly using an electric mixer fitted with a dough hook (the dough can be left to rise overnight in the refrigerator). You can vary the flavor and texture by chopping the chocolate very finely or into larger chunks.

petites brioches

3¼ cups all-purpose flour, plus extra for dusting

1 teaspoon salt

7 tablespoons unsalted butter, cut into small pieces

¼ cup sugar

1 cup plus 2 tablespoons milk, lukewarm

½ oz. cake compressed yeast or 1 package (¼ oz.) active dry yeast*

1 extra large egg, beaten

1 teaspoon vanilla extract

5½ oz. bittersweet chocolate, finely or coarsely chopped

⅓ cup pine nuts, lightly toasted

1 egg, beaten, to glaze

12 individual brioche molds, 3 inches diameter, or 2 medium brioche molds, 6½ inches diameter, or 2 loaf pans, 1 lb. each, well buttered

Makes 12 tiny brioches or 2 medium brioches or loaves

* To use active dry yeast, add one ¼ oz. package to the flour with the sugar and mix well. Add the liquids and finish as in main recipe.

Put the flour and salt into a large mixing bowl and stir well. Add the butter and, using the tips of your fingers, rub into the flour until the mixture resembles bread crumbs. Stir in the sugar,* then make a well in the center.

Put the milk into a bowl and crumble the compressed yeast over the top. Stir until smooth, then stir in the egg and vanilla extract. Pour the mixture into the well in the flour. Using the dough hook of an electric mixer and low speed, gradually mix the flour into the liquids to make a soft and slightly sticky dough. On low speed, knead the dough for about 5 minutes or until smooth, elastic, shiny, and soft. If the dough still sticks to the sides of the bowl, work in a little extra flour, 1 tablespoon at a time.

If making the dough by hand, put it onto a well-floured work surface and knead for 10 minutes until smooth, elastic, and shiny. If it is difficult to work, add a little extra flour.

Return the dough to the cleaned-out bowl, then slip it into a large plastic bag and let rise in a warm place until doubled in size—1½ hours, or overnight in the refrigerator.

Punch down the dough with your knuckles and invert onto a floured work surface. Pat out to a large rectangle, then sprinkle with the chocolate and pine nuts. Fold or roll up, flatten, and repeat twice until the chocolate and nuts are evenly distributed.

Cut the dough into 12 even portions for individual brioches or into 2 for large ones. Shape the 12 portions into balls and put one into each mold. For large ones, cut one-quarter off each portion of dough for the top and set aside. Shape the larger piece into a ball and put into the mold. Using 2 fingers, make a hole in the center. Roll the smaller piece of dough into a ball, then into an egg shape. Push the narrow end into the hole. For a loaf, scoop the dough into the pans. Put into a plastic bag and let rise in a warm place until doubled in size—1 hour, or overnight in the refrigerator.

Uncover the dough, brush with beaten egg, then bake in a preheated oven at 400°F until well risen and golden brown—15 minutes for individual brioches, 35 minutes for large ones. Invert onto a wire rack and let cool. Eat warm.

Can be frozen for up to 1 month.

confections

I can't stop myself smiling when something chocolate appears on
the table to round off a meal. Tarts and pies, mousses and soufflés—
there's a chocolate confection for every season (and, if you use really
good unsweetened cocoa powder, it will deliver real flavor without
any extra sugar or fat).

very rich chocolate brûlée

Steve Painter, fellow chocolate fiend and the designer of this book, insisted I include this recipe, which he makes often. The smooth chocolate cream can be made up to two days ahead, with the crunchy caramel topping added just before serving. You need a very hot broiler or a cook's blowtorch, available from kitchen suppliers (page 126) for the best mirror-like finish.

2½ cups heavy cream

1 vanilla bean, split lengthwise*

10 oz. bittersweet chocolate, chopped

4 extra large egg yolks

½ cup confectioners' sugar, sifted

about 1/4 cup sugar, for sprinkling

8 small soufflé dishes or ramekins, 2/3 cup each

a bain-marie or roasting pan

Serves 8

Pour the cream into a heavy saucepan and add the vanilla bean. Heat gently until just too hot for your finger to bear. Cover with a lid and leave to infuse for about 30 minutes.

Lift out the vanilla bean and, using a tip of a knife, scrape the seeds into the cream. Gently reheat the cream, then remove from the heat and stir in the chopped chocolate. When melted and smooth, let cool slightly.

Meanwhile, put the egg yolks and the confectioners' sugar into a mixing bowl, beat with a wooden spoon until well blended, then stir in the just-warm chocolate cream. Pour into the soufflé dishes, then stand the dishes in a bain-marie (a roasting pan half-filled with warm water). Cook in a preheated oven at 350°F for about 30 minutes until just firm. Remove from the bain-marie and let cool, then cover and chill overnight or for up to 48 hours.

When ready to serve, heat the broiler to maximum and half-fill the bain-marie or roasting pan with ice cubes and water. Sprinkle the tops of the chocolate creams with sugar, then set the soufflé dishes in the icy water (this prevents the chocolate melting) and quickly flash under the broiler or with a blowtorch until the sugar melts and caramelizes. Eat within 1 hour.

Note The vanilla bean can be replaced with 1 tablespoon dark rum, added to the mixture at the same time as the egg yolks.

nut and chocolate strudel

An irresistible combination of crisp phyllo, nuts, and rich dark chocolate makes this dessert a firm favorite at every dinner party. Serve with plenty of whipped cream. For best results, use only good-quality chocolate and very fresh nuts and, before using the phyllo pastry dough, make sure it's properly thawed out, according to the instructions on the package.

¾ cup blanched almonds

1 cup shelled unsalted pistachios

1 cup walnut pieces

5 tablespoons unsalted butter

scant ½ cup firmly packed light brown sugar

3 oz. bittersweet chocolate

7 oz. phyllo pastry dough, thawed if frozen

whipped cream, to serve

Cinnamon syrup

½ cup sugar

1 cinnamon stick

1 teaspoon lemon juice

2 tablespoons honey

a large roasting pan, well buttered

Serves 6–8

Put all the nuts into a food processor and chop until they resemble coarse bread crumbs. Put the nuts into a heavy, dry skillet and stir over low heat until just starting to color. Because nuts scorch quickly, it's best to undercook slightly, rather than risk overcooking them. Remove from the heat and stir in the butter and sugar. Let cool. Using a sharp knife, chop the chocolate the same size as the chopped nuts, then mix with the nuts.

Unwrap the phyllo pastry dough and put onto a clean work surface. Overlap the sheets to make a large rectangle about 36 x 24 inches.

Sprinkle the filling evenly over the phyllo, then carefully roll up. Arrange in a horseshoe shape in the prepared roasting pan, tucking the ends under neatly. Bake in a preheated oven at 350°F for about 25 minutes or until the top is crisp and light golden brown. Remove from the oven and let cool in the pan while making the syrup.

To make the cinnamon syrup, put the sugar and a scant ½ cup water into a heavy saucepan and heat gently, stirring frequently, until dissolved. Bring to a boil, then add the cinnamon stick, lemon juice, and honey and simmer for 10 minutes until syrupy. Let cool for 5 minutes, then remove the cinnamon stick and pour the hot syrup over the strudel. Let cool so the strudel can absorb the syrup, then cut into thick slices and serve with piles of whipped cream.

Best eaten within 24 hours. Not suitable for freezing.

easy chocolate and berry roulade

A splendid stand-by dessert for a special dinner when time is tight. The roulade is a simple all-in-one cake mix, made with an electric mixer or hand beaters, baked in 8 minutes, and filled with crème fraîche or cream mixed with preserves and fresh berries.

½ cup sugar

2 extra large eggs

4 tablespoons unsalted butter, very soft

½ cup self-rising flour

3 tablespoons unsweetened cocoa powder

1 teaspoon vanilla extract

Cream filling

¼ cup blackberry preserves*

1 cup plus 2 tablespoons heavy cream, whipped, or crème fraîche

8 oz. fresh blackberries, about 2 cups, picked over to clean*

To serve

confectioners' sugar, for sprinkling

chocolate curls (page 15)

a jelly roll pan or baking tray, about 12 x 8 inches, buttered and lined with nonstick parchment paper

Serves 6–8

Vary the fruit, depending on what's available – try pitted black cherries, raspberries, blueberries, strawberries, all with matching preserves.

1 Put the sugar, eggs, and butter into a mixing bowl, or the bowl of an electric mixer. Sift the flour and cocoa into the bowl, then add the vanilla extract and 2 tablespoons warm water.

2 Beat for about 1 minute or until you have a smooth, thick, creamy cake batter.

3 Pour the mixture into the prepared pan.

4 Spread it evenly with a spatula.

5 Bake in a preheated oven at 400°F for 8 minutes or until the mixture is well risen and just springy when you press it with your finger. Let cool in the pan for about 1 minute.

6 Put a sheet of nonstick parchment paper on the work surface and sprinkle heavily with confectioners' sugar.

7 Invert the sponge onto the parchment paper, then peel off the paper used to line the pan.

8 Carefully roll up the sponge with the paper inside, like a jelly roll. Cover with the damp dish cloth and leave on the wire rack until completely cold.

9 Put the preserves and whipped cream or crème fraîche into a mixing bowl and, using a metal spoon, fold gently together.

10 Carefully unroll the sponge. Don't worry if it has cracked—it will still look and taste good.

11 Spread the cream mixture over the sponge.

12 Sprinkle the berries evenly over the top.

13 Roll up the sponge fairly loosely and set on a large serving plate. Cover and chill until ready to serve—I prefer the texture the next day.

14 Just before serving, sprinkle with confectioners' sugar and decorate with chocolate curls.

Best eaten within 48 hours. Not suitable for freezing.

These thick, crisp batter cakes are cooked by street vendors in Holland (the name comes from the Dutch *wafel*), Belgium, and Northern France (where they are called *gaufres*). Pilgrims from Northern Europe took the recipe to America, where waffle parties became very popular in the 18th century. The honeycomb or grid pattern of the waffle is perfect for holding lashings of whipped cream, maple syrup, melted butter, or peanut butter. My recipe comes from my American husband's family where, apparently, it has been made most weekends for 75 years. My son invented the chocolate version. You will need an electric or stove-top waffle iron for cooking these waffles.

chocolate waffles

1½ cups all-purpose flour

a good pinch of salt

½ cup unsweetened cocoa powder

2 teaspoons baking powder

3½ tablespoons sugar

2 extra large eggs, separated

1¾ cups milk

1 teaspoon vanilla extract

3 tablespoons unsalted butter, melted

confectioners' sugar, for sprinkling

a waffle iron or electric waffle maker, well buttered (see recipe method)

Makes 10 waffles, about 6 inches across

Grease the waffle iron or electric waffle maker (consult the manufacturer's instructions if using for the first time), then heat. Depending on the type of waffle maker* or waffle iron, it may be necessary to brush it well again with oil or melted butter using a non-plastic brush.

Sift the flour, salt, cocoa, baking powder, and sugar into a mixing bowl and make a well in the center. Add the egg yolks, milk, vanilla extract, and melted butter to the well and, using a whisk, beat until just blended. Then gradually beat the dry mixture into the liquids to make a thick, smooth batter.

Put the egg whites into a spotlessly clean, greasefree bowl and, using electric or rotary beaters, beat until stiff peaks form. Using a large metal spoon, fold the egg whites into the batter until it looks evenly foamy—it is better to have streaks than to overmix at this point.

Using the large metal spoon, spoon in enough batter to fill the hot waffle iron, then close. Cook for 30 seconds over medium heat, then turn over the iron and cook the other side in the same way. Serve hot from the iron, sprinkled with plenty of confectioners' sugar.

*Note If using an electric waffle maker, follow the manufacturer's guidelines, but note that chocolate waffles will scorch quicker than plain ones.

An individual white chocolate sponge dessert, baked with a hidden center of molten chocolate and served with whipped cream or a chocolate sauce (page 106), is perfect for any occasion. It is very important to use the best quality white and bittersweet chocolate you can find.

white and black desserts

Dark chocolate filling

3 oz. bittersweet chocolate, chopped

⅓ cup heavy cream

White chocolate sponge

3½ oz. white chocolate, chopped

1½ sticks unsalted butter, at room temperature

¾ cup sugar

3 extra large eggs, beaten

1⅔ cups self-rising flour

a pinch of salt

½ teaspoon vanilla extract

about ¼ cup milk

an ice cube tray, oiled

6 small dessert molds,
2¾ inches diameter, well buttered

Serves 6

The chocolate filling should be made at least 1 hour before making the sponge (though the filling can be kept in the freezer for up to 1 week). Put the chocolate into a heatproof bowl set over a saucepan of steaming but not boiling water and melt gently (do not let the base of the bowl touch the water). Remove the bowl from the heat and stir gently until just smooth. Stir in the cream, then pour into the prepared ice cube tray to make 6 "cubes." Freeze for at least 1 hour.

When ready to make the dessert, put the white chocolate into a heatproof bowl set over a saucepan of steaming but not boiling water and melt gently (do not let the base of the bowl touch the water). Remove the bowl from the heat and stir gently until just smooth, then let cool.

Put the butter into a large mixing bowl and, using a wooden spoon or electric mixer, beat the butter until creamy, then gradually beat in the sugar. When the mixture is very light and fluffy, beat in the eggs 1 tablespoon at a time, beating well after each addition. Using a large metal spoon, carefully fold in the flour and salt, followed by the melted chocolate, vanilla extract, and just enough milk to give the mixture a firm dropping consistency. Spoon the mixture into the prepared molds to fill by about half. Turn out the dark chocolate cubes, put one into the center of each mold, then top up with more sponge mixture so each one is three-quarters full.

Stand the molds in a roasting pan, then cover loosely with well-buttered foil. Bake in a preheated oven at 350°F for about 25 minutes or until just firm to the touch. Run a round-bladed knife inside each mold to loosen the edges, then carefully invert onto individual plates. Serve immediately.

This delicious soufflé, with its exceedingly light and meltingly soft texture, is more like a hot chocolate mousse. The recipe is easy though—if you can make meringue you can make this soufflé. Serve with crisp cookies, such as the Crescent Moons on page 64.

chocolate soufflé

6 oz. bittersweet chocolate, chopped

²⁄₃ cup heavy cream

3 extra large eggs, separated

2 tablespoons Cognac or brandy

2 large egg whites

about 1 tablespoon softened butter, for the soufflé dishes

3 tablespoons sugar, plus extra for the soufflé dishes

confectioners' sugar, for sprinkling

4 soufflé dishes, 1¹⁄₂ cups each, or 4 large coffee cups, buttered and sugared (see recipe method)

a baking tray or roasting pan

Serves 4

Brush the soufflé dishes with a little melted butter, then sprinkle with sugar to give an even coating. Stand the dishes on a baking tray or in a roasting pan.

Put the chocolate into a heavy saucepan, pour in the cream, then set over very low heat and stir frequently until melted and smooth. Remove from the heat and stir in the egg yolks, one at a time, followed by the Cognac. At this point the mixture can be covered and set aside for up to 2 hours.

Put the 5 egg whites into a spotlessly clean, greasefree bowl and, using electric beaters or mixer, beat until stiff peaks form. Gradually beat in the sugar to give a glossy, stiff meringue. The chocolate mixture should feel comfortably warm to your finger, so gently reheat if necessary. Using a large metal spoon, add a little of the meringue to the chocolate mixture and mix thoroughly. This loosens the consistency, making it easier to incorporate the rest of the meringue. Pour the chocolate mixture on top of the remaining meringue and gently fold both mixtures together until just blended.

Spoon or pour the mixture into the prepared soufflé dishes—the mixture should come to just below the rim. Bake in a preheated oven at 425°F for 8–10 minutes until barely set—the centers should be soft, and wobble when gently shaken. Sprinkle with confectioners' sugar and eat immediately.

Variations

Chocolate, Prune, and Armagnac Soufflé Omit the Cognac. Substitute 8 large pitted prunes soaked overnight in ¹⁄₄ cup Armagnac. Chop the prunes coarsely, then stir them, and any remaining liquid, into the chocolate mixture.

Chocolate Amaretti Soufflé Omit the Cognac. Set an amaretti cookie into each prepared soufflé dish. Spoon over 1 teaspoon Amaretto liqueur, then add the chocolate soufflé mixture and bake as in the main recipe.

classic chocolate mousse

This French classic, still enjoyed in bistros, elegant restaurants, and homes, relies on just three ingredients—the finest chocolate you can find, the freshest eggs, and unsalted butter. Serve in pretty glasses or coffee cups, with crisp cookies or Tiny Florentines (page 24).

3 oz. bittersweet chocolate, finely chopped

2 tablespoons water, brandy, or rum

2 teaspoons unsalted butter, at room temperature

3 extra large eggs, separated

4 serving bowls, coffee cups, or glasses

Serves 4

Put the chocolate and water, brandy, or rum into a heatproof bowl set over a saucepan of steaming but not boiling water and leave until just melted (do not let the base of the bowl touch the water). Remove the bowl from the heat and gently stir in the butter (it is vital to melt the chocolate gently without letting it get too hot, and to stir as little as possible). Leave for 1 minute, then gently stir in the egg yolks, one at a time.

Put the egg whites into a spotlessly clean, greasefree bowl and, using electric beaters or mixer, beat until stiff peaks form. Stir about one-quarter of the egg whites into the chocolate mixture to loosen it, then, using a large metal spoon, gently fold in the rest of the egg whites in 3 batches. Carefully spoon into serving bowls, cups, or glasses, then chill for 2 hours before serving.

Best eaten within 12 hours. Not suitable for freezing.

Variations

Espresso Mousse Make the recipe above, replacing the water or brandy with 3 tablespoons good-quality espresso coffee, and beating 3 tablespoons sugar into the stiff egg whites before adding them to the chocolate mixture.

Cappuccino Mousse This is a creamy version of the espresso mousse above. Put 1/2 cup heavy or whipping cream into a mixing bowl and, using electric beaters or mixer, whip until soft peaks form. Fold half the cream into the mousse after the egg whites, then spoon into small coffee cups and chill for 2 hours. Just before serving, spoon the rest of the cream on top of the mousse, then sprinkle with cocoa.

Linzertorte is a classic dish dating back to the glory days of the Austrian Empire, and traditionally made from a nutty shortbread-like pastry dough and raspberry preserves. This recipe is not authentic, but fresh raspberries are the perfect contrast to the ultra-rich crust. Serve with vanilla ice cream or whipped cream.

fresh raspberry chocolate linzertorte

8 oz. hazelnuts (2 cups chopped)

1 stick unsalted butter, at room temperature

¾ cup firmly packed confectioners' sugar, sifted, plus extra for sprinkling

3 extra large egg yolks

1½ cups all-purpose flour

½ teaspoon baking powder

2 teaspoons ground cinnamon

¼ teaspoon grated nutmeg

¼ cup unsweetened cocoa powder

Raspberry filling

1½ tablespoons cornstarch

3 tablespoons sugar, or to taste

1¼ lb. fresh raspberries, black raspberries, or blueberries

a false-bottom tart pan, 9–9½ inches diameter, well buttered

Serves 8

Put the hazelnuts into an ovenproof dish and toast in a preheated oven at 350°F for about 15 minutes or until light golden brown. If the nuts still have their papery brown skins, put them in a clean, dry dish cloth, then gather up the ends and rub the nuts together to loosen the skins. Let cool, then transfer the skinned nuts to a food processor and grind to a fine powder.

Put the butter into a mixing bowl and, using a wooden spoon or electric mixer, beat until creamy. Add the confectioners' sugar and beat, slowly at first, until light and fluffy. Beat in the egg yolks one at a time, beating well after each addition. Sift the flour, baking powder, cinnamon, nutmeg, and cocoa onto the mixture and work in using a wooden spoon. Finally add the ground nuts and work in, using your hands to bring the dough together.

Take three-quarters of the dough and crumble it into the prepared pan. Using your fingers, press the dough over the base and up the sides to cover the inside of the pan completely and form a layer about ½ inch thick. Chill for 15 minutes. Put the remaining dough onto a well floured work surface and roll out, slightly thinner, to a rectangle about 9 x 6 inches. Cut into strips about ½ inch wide.

Sprinkle the cornstarch and sugar over the raspberries and toss gently until almost mixed. Transfer the filling into the pie crust and spread gently and evenly.

Arrange the lattice strips over the filling—if the dough breaks, just push it back together again. Bake in the preheated oven at 350°F for 25–30 minutes until the dough is a slightly darker brown and just firm. Let cool, then remove from the pan and serve sprinkled with confectioners' sugar.

Best eaten the same day. Not suitable for freezing.

Chocolate lovers in Italy are well served in Piedmont, in the far northwest. The capital city, Turin, is a veritable heaven-on-earth with irresistible pastry shops on every corner. One famous delight are *gianduiotti*, chocolates made with dark chocolate and toasted hazelnuts. This torta also comes from Turin, but other recipes from the region are made with almonds or walnuts and flavored with brandy, rum, or grated orange zest. Use very fresh nuts for the best flavor.

italian chocolate and hazelnut torta

3½ oz. hazelnuts, about 1 cup

3½ oz. plain butter cookies, such as Petit Beurre

3½ oz. bittersweet chocolate, finely chopped

1 extra large egg, at room temperature

1 extra large egg yolk, at room temperature

3 tablespoons sugar

5 tablespoons unsalted butter

unsweetened cocoa powder, for sprinkling

whipped cream or ice cream, to serve

a springform cake pan, 8 inches diameter, lightly buttered and bottom lined with parchment paper

an ovenproof dish or baking tray

Serves 6–8

Put the hazelnuts into an ovenproof dish or onto a baking tray and toast them in a preheated oven at 400°F for 5 minutes or until lightly browned (watch them carefully as they will taste bitter if they become too dark). If the hazelnuts still have their papery brown skins, put them in a clean, dry dish cloth, then gather up the ends and rub the nuts together to remove the skins. Leave the skinned nuts to cool, then chop very coarsely.

Put the cookies into a food processor and pulse until coarse crumbs form. Alternatively, put the cookies into a plastic bag and crush with a rolling pin.

Put the chocolate into a heatproof bowl set over a saucepan of steaming but not boiling water and melt gently (do not let the base of the bowl touch the water).

Meanwhile, put the whole egg, egg yolk, and sugar into a mixing bowl and, using an electric mixer, electric beaters, or rotary beaters, beat vigorously until the mixture is very pale, thick, and mousse-like—when the beaters are lifted, a thick ribbon-like trail slowly falls back into the bowl. Heat the butter in a small, heavy saucepan until just bubbling. Pour the hot butter onto the mixture in a thin, steady stream while still beating at top speed (this is not so easy with a rotary beater), then beat in the melted chocolate. Using a large metal spoon, gently fold in the chopped nuts and crushed cookies. When thoroughly mixed, pour the mixture into the prepared pan, spreading it gently and evenly. Cover the top of the pan with plastic wrap, then chill for at least 3 hours or overnight, until firm.

To serve, unclip the pan and remove the torta. Set on a serving plate, sprinkle with cocoa, and serve, well chilled, with whipped cream or ice cream.

Best eaten within 5 days. Do not freeze.

A delicious finale for a lovely summertime dinner, serve this
very light cake with piles of berries and whipped cream.

italian chocolate amaretto torta

4 oz. bittersweet chocolate, chopped

2 tablespoons Amaretto liqueur (optional)

1 stick unsalted butter,
at room temperature

½ cup plus 1 tablespoon sugar

3 extra large eggs, separated

2 oz. (about 10) amaretti cookies, crushed

½ cup all-purpose flour, sifted,
plus extra for flouring

To serve

whipped cream

blueberries, raspberries,
or baked apricots

*a false-bottom cake pan,
8 inches diameter, buttered,
bottom lined with parchment
paper, then floured*

Serves 8

Put the chocolate and Amaretto into a heatproof bowl set over a saucepan of steaming but not boiling water and leave until melted (do not let the base of the bowl touch the water). Remove the bowl from the heat, stir gently, and let cool.

Put the butter and the ½ cup sugar into a mixing bowl and, using a wooden spoon or electric mixer, beat until very light and fluffy. Beat in the egg yolks one at a time, then stir in the cooled chocolate. When thoroughly blended, use a large metal spoon to fold in the crushed cookies and flour.

Put the egg whites into a spotlessly clean, greasefree bowl and, using electric beaters or mixer, beat until stiff peaks form. Beat in the remaining 1 tablespoon sugar to make a stiff, glossy meringue, then fold into the cake mixture in 3 batches.

Transfer the mixture to the prepared pan and bake in a preheated oven at 350°F for 30–35 minutes until just firm to the touch. Let cool in the pan for 10 minutes. Remove from the pan and transfer to a wire rack to cool completely.

Sprinkle with confectioners' sugar and serve slightly warm or at room temperature with whipped cream and fresh berries. Alternatively, sprinkle halved apricots with a little sugar, Amaretto, and crushed amaretti, bake until soft, then serve with the torta.

Best eaten within 3 days. Not suitable for freezing.

black cherry frangipane pie

Almonds, cherries, and chocolate work so well together—the flavors and textures bring out the best in each other. Serve with vanilla ice cream, sour cream, or crème fraîche.

1 cup plus 2 tablespoons all-purpose flour, plus extra for dusting

a pinch of salt

1 tablespoon sugar

1 stick unsalted butter, chilled and cut into small pieces

ice cream or sour cream, to serve

Almond filling

1 stick plus 1 tablespoon unsalted butter, at room temperature

2/3 cup sugar

2 extra large eggs, beaten

2 teaspoons kirsch or 1 teaspoon almond extract

4 oz. (1 cup firmly packed) slivered almonds, finely ground in a food processor

3 tablespoons all-purpose flour

3 oz. bittersweet chocolate, finely chopped, plus 1½ oz. melted, to finish

14 oz. black or red cherries, pitted, about 1½ cups

a false-bottom pie pan, 9 inches diameter, buttered

parchment paper and baking beans or dried beans

Serves 6–8

1 To make the dough in a food processor, put the flour, salt, sugar, and butter into the bowl and process until the mixture resembles fine crumbs. With the machine running, add 3 tablespoons ice water through the feed tube, then process until the dough comes together. If there are dry crumbs, add a little more water, 1 tablespoon at a time, until you have a slightly firm dough. Wrap and chill for 15 minutes.

Alternatively, to make the dough by hand, sift the flour, salt, and sugar into a mixing bowl. Add the pieces of butter and, using the tips of your fingers, rub into the flour. When the mixture resembles bread crumbs, use a round-bladed knife to stir in 3 tablespoons ice water to make a firm dough. Wrap and chill for 15 minutes.

2 Put the dough onto a lightly floured work surface and, using a rolling pin, roll out the dough to a large round, about 11 inches diameter.

3 Carefully lift the dough with the rolling pin and drape it over the prepared pie pan.

Preheat the oven to 375°F.

4 Press the dough into the corners and fluting. Roll the pin over the top of the pan to cut off the excess dough.

5 Prick the base all over with a fork, then chill for 15 minutes.

6 Line the pie crust with a piece of parchment paper a little larger than the circle of pastry. Fill with baking beans or dried beans to hold the paper down, then bake in the preheated oven at 375°F for 10 minutes. This is called "baking blind."

7 Remove the paper and beans and bake for a further 5 minutes to dry out the base. Remove from the oven and let cool.

8 To make the filling, put the butter and sugar into a mixing bowl and, using a wooden spoon or electric mixer, beat until light and fluffy.

9 Gradually beat in the eggs and kirsch.

10 Using a large metal spoon, fold in the ground almonds and flour.

11 Scatter the chopped chocolate over the base of the pie crust.

Top with an even layer of cherries.

12 Spoon the almond mixture on top and spread evenly. Bake in a preheated oven at 375°F for about 30 minutes until golden brown and firm to the touch. Remove from the oven, let cool on a wire rack, then carefully remove from the pan.

13 To finish, drizzle the melted chocolate over the top with a fork, then leave to set. Serve at room temperature with vanilla ice cream, sour cream, or crème fraîche.

Best eaten within 3 days. Not suitable for freezing.

This slightly unusual cheesecake from Italy—very light in texture yet full of flavor—can be eaten warm or at room temperature. Mascarpone is an Italian cheese made from thick, fresh cream, which has not been left to ripen or ferment—this gives it a slightly sweet taste and an extremely rich texture.

warm chocolate mascarpone cheesecake

Cookie base

8 oz. graham crackers or digestive biscuits, about 2⅔ cups

4 tablespoons unsalted butter

2 oz. bittersweet chocolate, finely chopped

Chocolate filling

2 extra large eggs, separated

a scant ½ cup sugar

8 oz. mascarpone cheese

⅔ cup heavy cream, lightly whipped

1¾ oz. chocolate, very finely chopped

¼ cup unsweetened cocoa powder, sifted

1 cup slivered almonds, finely ground in a food processor, or ½ cup almond flour

1–2 tablespoons Amaretto liqueur or brandy

confectioners' sugar, for sprinkling

ice cream or thick cream, to serve

a springform cake pan, 9 inches diameter, well buttered

Serves 8

To make the base, put the crackers into a food processor and pulse until fine crumbs form. Alternatively, put the cookies into a plastic bag and crush with a rolling pin. Transfer the crumbs into a mixing bowl. Put the butter and chocolate into a heatproof bowl set over a saucepan of steaming but not boiling water and melt gently (do not let the base of the bowl touch the water). Remove from the heat, stir gently, then stir into the cookie crumbs. When well mixed, transfer the mixture to the prepared pan and, using the back of a spoon, press onto the base and about halfway up the sides of the pan. Chill while making the filling.

To make the filling, put the egg yolks and sugar into a large mixing bowl and, using electric beaters or mixer, beat until very thick and mousse-like—when the beaters are lifted, a wide ribbon-like trail slowly falls back into the bowl. Put the mascarpone into a separate bowl, beat until smooth, then gently fold in the whipped cream.

Gently stir the mascarpone mixture into the egg yolks, then add the chopped chocolate, cocoa, ground almonds, and liqueur and mix gently.

Put the egg whites into a spotlessly clean, greasefree bowl and, using electric beaters or mixer, beat until stiff peaks form. Using a large metal spoon, fold the egg whites into the mixture in 3 batches.

Pour the filling into the cookie crust and bake in a preheated oven at 325°F for about 1 hour or until set and beginning to color. Remove from the oven and let cool for about 20 minutes, then carefully unclip and remove the pan. Sprinkle with confectioners' sugar and serve warm or at room temperature with ice cream or thick cream.

This famous pie hails from the South—it is supposed to look like the thick, dark, muddy waters of the Mississippi Delta. It is very easy to make and perfect to share with family and friends.

mississippi mud pie

Cookie base

8 oz. graham crackers or digestive biscuits, about 2²/₃ cups

4 tablespoons unsalted butter

2 oz. bittersweet chocolate, finely chopped

Chocolate filling

6 oz. bittersweet chocolate, chopped

1½ sticks unsalted butter, cut into small pieces

4 extra large eggs, beaten

½ cup firmly packed light brown sugar

½ cup firmly packed dark brown sugar

1¾ cup heavy cream

Chocolate cream

²/₃ cup heavy cream, well chilled

3 tablespoons unsweetened cocoa powder

⅓ cup confectioners' sugar

a springform cake pan, 9 inches diameter, well buttered

Serves 8

To make the base, put the crackers into a food processor and process until fine crumbs form. Alternatively, put the crackers into a plastic bag and crush with a rolling pin. Transfer the crumbs to a mixing bowl.

Put the butter and chocolate into a heatproof bowl set over a saucepan of steaming but not boiling water and melt gently (do not let the base of the bowl touch the water). Remove from the heat, stir gently, then stir into the cracker crumbs. When well mixed, transfer the mixture to the prepared pan and, using the back of a spoon, press onto the base and about halfway up the sides of the pan. Chill while making the filling.

To make the filling, put the chocolate and butter into a heatproof bowl set over a saucepan of steaming but not boiling water and melt gently (do not let the base of the bowl touch the water). Remove from the heat, stir gently, then let cool.

Put the eggs and sugar into a large mixing bowl and, using electric beaters or mixer, beat until thick and foamy. Beat in the cream followed by the melted chocolate. Pour the mixture into the cookie crust and bake in a preheated oven at 350°F for about 45 minutes until just firm. Let cool for a few minutes, then remove from the pan.

To make the chocolate cream, put the cream into a mixing bowl, then sift the cocoa and confectioners' sugar on top and stir gently with a wooden spoon until blended. Cover and chill for 2 hours.

Serve the pie at room temperature with the chocolate cream. The pie can be made up to 2 days in advance and kept well covered in the refrigerator. Remove from the refrigerator 30 minutes before serving.

sticky chocolate pecan pie

Incredibly rich and gooey, this is a real treat. The short, crumbly dough is simple to make in a food processor, and the filling has a wonderfully fudgy taste and texture. Use a freshly opened package of pecans for best results.

1½ cups all-purpose flour, plus extra for dusting

a pinch of salt

1 tablespoon sugar

1 stick unsalted butter, chilled and cut into small pieces

1 extra large egg yolk mixed with 1 tablespoon cold water

vanilla ice cream or whipped cream, to serve

Chocolate filling

3 tablespoons unsalted butter, softened

¾ cup firmly packed light brown sugar

⅔ cup corn syrup or golden syrup

3 extra large eggs, beaten

1 teaspoon vanilla extract

3½ oz. bittersweet chocolate, melted

1 cup pecans

a false-bottom tart pan, 9 inches diameter, well buttered

parchment paper and baking beans or dried beans

Serves 8

To make the dough in a food processor, put the flour, salt, sugar, and butter into the bowl and process until the mixture looks like fine crumbs. With the machine running, add the egg yolk and water through the feed tube. Run the machine until the dough comes together. If there are dry crumbs, add a teaspoon or so extra water.

If making the dough by hand, sift the flour, salt, and sugar into a large mixing bowl. Add the butter and rub in using the tips of your fingers. When the mixture looks like crumbs, stir in the yolk mixture with a round-bladed knife to make a firm dough. Wrap and chill for 15 minutes until firm.

Put the dough onto a floured work surface and, using a rolling pin, roll out to a large circle about 2 inches larger than the tart pan, then use to line the pan. Prick the base of the pie crust with a fork, then chill for 15 minutes.

Line the pie crust with a sheet of nonstick parchment paper, then fill with baking beans or dried beans. Bake "blind" in a preheated oven at 350°F for about 12 minutes, then carefully remove the paper and beans. Bake for a further 10 minutes until lightly golden and just firm. Remove from the oven and let cool while making the filling.

Put the butter, sugar, and corn syrup into a mixing bowl and, using a wooden spoon or electric mixer, beat until smooth. Gradually beat in the eggs and then the vanilla extract. Stir in the melted chocolate followed by the pecans.

Pour the mixture into the prepared pie crust and bake in a preheated oven at 350°F for 35 minutes until just firm to the touch. Remove from the oven and let cool—the filling will sink slightly. Serve warm or at room temperature with vanilla ice cream or whipped cream.

Best eaten within 4 days.

chocolate fondue

4 oz. bittersweet chocolate, chopped

4 oz. white chocolate, chopped

4 oz. milk chocolate, chopped

⅔ cup heavy cream

1 tablespoon white rum or
Grand Marnier (optional)

To serve

1 small pineapple

2 medium bananas

4 oz. strawberries

4 oz. cherries

2 medium pears

*a fondue set, small saucepans,
or heatproof bowls*

Serves 4–6

This recipe comes from Michael Levy of Le Chocolatier in Great Barrow, near Chester in England—one of the world's most renowned factories, specializing in "couture" chocolate. It is a very simple idea for creating a marvelous special-occasion dessert. Buy the chocolate you most like to eat—there is a huge variety of brands and types available. Use small saucepans or heatproof bowls set on the table over a warming tray or three candle-warmers—and have lots of fun.

Put each type of chocolate into small, heatproof bowls set over small saucepans of steaming but not boiling water and melt gently (do not let the base of the bowls touch the water).

Put the cream into a separate saucepan, bring to a boil, then add 3 tablespoons to each saucepan or bowl of melted chocolate and mix gently. If using white rum or Grand Marnier, add it to the white chocolate mixture.

Set the saucepans or bowls over the lowest possible heat on a warming tray in the center of the table, surrounded by the fruit. Cut the fruit at the table and immediately dip into the melted chocolate fondues and eat.

chocolate sauces

rich dark chocolate sauce

For a creamy sauce, use light cream instead of water or, for a flavored sauce, replace some of the water with a tablespoon or so of brandy, rum, or coffee liqueur.

4 oz. bittersweet chocolate, finely chopped
6 tablespoons unsalted butter, cut into small pieces

Serves 4–6

Put the chopped chocolate, butter, and 1/2 cup water into a heatproof bowl set over a saucepan of steaming but not boiling water (do not let the base of the bowl touch the water). Stir frequently until melted and very smooth.

Remove from the heat and stir well until glossy and slightly thickened. As the sauce cools, it will become even thicker. Serve warm.

creamy chocolate sauce

A very quick, rich sauce for ice cream, profiteroles, and other desserts. Just before serving it can be flavored with rum, brandy, or coffee liqueur. For a slightly thinner, less rich sauce, use light cream, or cream mixed half and half with milk or coffee.

1/2 cup heavy cream
3 oz. bittersweet chocolate, finely chopped
1/2 teaspoon vanilla extract

Serves 4–6

Put the cream into a small, heavy saucepan and heat gently, stirring frequently. When the cream comes to a boil, remove from the heat. Let cool for 1 minute, then stir in the chopped chocolate. Stir gently until the sauce is smooth. Stir in the vanilla extract and serve immediately.

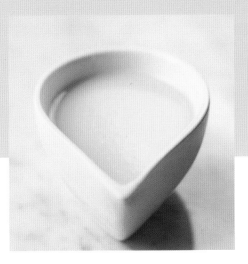

chocolate custard sauce

The classic sauce for steamed desserts.

2 cups whole milk

3 tablespoons unsweetened cocoa powder

1/3 cup sugar

1 tablespoon cornstarch

2 large egg yolks

Serves 4–6

Put all but 2 tablespoons of the milk into a large, heavy saucepan and heat until almost boiling. Sift the cocoa, sugar, and cornstarch into a heatproof bowl, stir in the egg yolks and the 2 tablespoons cold milk to form a thick paste, then stir in the hot milk. Strain the mixture back into the saucepan and stir constantly over low heat until the mixture thickens—do not let the mixture boil or it will curdle.

Remove from the heat and use immediately, or keep it warm until ready to serve.

white chocolate sauce

The flavor depends on the quality of the white chocolate, so use the best you can lay your hands on rather than chocolate candy bars.

7 oz. good-quality white chocolate, finely chopped

3/4 cup heavy cream

1/3 cup milk

Serves 4–6

Put the chocolate into a heatproof bowl set over a saucepan of steaming but not boiling water and melt gently (do not let the base of the bowl touch the water). Remove from the heat and stir gently until smooth.

Put the cream and milk into a small, heavy saucepan and heat until scalding hot, but not quite boiling. Remove from the heat. Pour the mixture onto the chocolate in a thin stream, beating constantly, to make a smooth sauce. Pour into a warmed pitcher and serve.

ice cream

The ultimate luxury on a hot day has to be freshly churned ice cream with crunchy wafers or crisp cones. A small, easy-to-use ice cream maker will pay for itself in a season. If you have to make these recipes by hand, just partially freeze the mixture, then beat with a fork. Repeat several times, then let freeze completely.

deluxe chocolate
ice cream

A truly rich and luxurious recipe—to make it even
richer, stir in some crushed praline (page 30) at the
same time as the cream.

7 oz. bittersweet chocolate, finely chopped

1¼ cups milk

1 large vanilla bean, split lengthwise

3 extra large egg yolks

⅓ cup sugar

¾ cup heavy cream, well chilled

an ice cream maker or freezer-proof container

Serves 4–6

Put the chocolate into a large bowl. Pour the milk into a heavy
saucepan and add the vanilla bean. Heat slowly over low heat,
stirring frequently, until the mixture is fairly hot—around 140°F,
then remove from the heat, cover, and leave to infuse for
15–20 minutes.

Put the egg yolks and sugar into a bowl and mix well. Add the
warm milk and mix thoroughly. Pour the mixture back into the
saucepan and stir over low heat until thick enough to coat the back
of a wooden spoon—don't let the mixture boil or it will curdle.

Remove the saucepan from the heat and discard the vanilla bean.
Pour the custard onto the chopped chocolate and stir until
smooth. Let cool, then cover and chill thoroughly. Put a bowl and
whisk into the refrigerator. When chilled, pour the cream into the
cold bowl and, using the whisk, whip until soft peaks form. Stir in
the chocolate custard.

Pour the mixture into an ice cream maker and churn until frozen.
Eat immediately or store in the freezer. Alternatively, put the mixture
into a freezer-proof container and freeze, stirring occasionally.

white chocolate
ice cream

The taste of this ice cream depends entirely on the
quality of the white chocolate. My favorite brands
are Lindt, and Green & Black Organic flavored with
vanilla—they are not too cloyingly sweet.

5½ oz. white chocolate, finely chopped

1 cup milk

1 cup heavy cream

1 vanilla bean, split lengthwise

4 extra large egg yolks

⅓ cup sugar

an ice cream maker or freezer-proof container

Serves 4–6

Put the chocolate into a large bowl. Pour the milk and cream into
a heavy saucepan, add the vanilla bean, and stir gently over low
heat until the milk is fairly hot—around 140°F—then remove from
the heat, cover, and leave to infuse for 15–20 minutes.

Put the egg yolks and sugar into a bowl and mix well. Add the hot
milk and stir well. Pour the mixture back into the saucepan and stir
over low heat until thick enough to coat the back of a wooden
spoon—don't let the mixture boil or it will curdle.

Remove the saucepan from the heat, discard the vanilla bean,
then let cool for 2 minutes. Pour the custard onto the chopped
chocolate and stir until smooth. Let cool, then cover and chill
thoroughly.

Pour the mixture into an ice cream maker and churn until frozen.
Eat immediately or store in the freezer. Alternatively, put the mixture
into a freezer-proof container and freeze, stirring occasionally.

pistachio and chocolate ice cream

Nobody makes pistachio ice cream like the Italians, but this home-style version is fairly authentic. Most supermarkets sell shelled unsalted pistachios—the roasted and salted snack kind aren't suitable for this recipe. Fresh nuts taste best, so use a fresh package.

¾ cup shelled unsalted pistachios

1 cup heavy cream, well chilled

1¼ cups milk

4 extra large egg yolks

½ cup sugar

3 oz. bittersweet chocolate, finely chopped

an ice cream maker or freezer-proof container

Serves 4–6

Put the pistachios and 3 tablespoons of the cream into a food processor or blender and process to a fine paste, scraping down the sides from time to time. Transfer the paste to a heavy saucepan and stir in the milk. Heat gently until almost boiling, stirring frequently, then remove from the heat, cover, and leave to infuse for 15–20 minutes.

Put the egg yolks and sugar into a bowl and mix well. Pour in the pistachio milk and stir well. Pour the mixture back into the saucepan. Stir gently over low heat until the mixture thickens—don't let it boil or it will curdle. Remove from the heat, pour into a clean bowl, let cool, then chill thoroughly. Put a bowl and whisk into the refrigerator to chill.

When ready to churn, put the rest of the cream into the chilled bowl and, using the whisk, whip until soft peaks form, then stir in the pistachio mixture and the chopped chocolate. Pour into an ice cream maker and churn until frozen. Eat immediately or store in the freezer. Alternatively, put the mixture into a freezer-proof container and freeze, stirring occasionally.

rich mocha ice cream

On a hot day, this is a great mid-morning reviver. I've tried this recipe made with all types of coffee—espresso, instant, concentrate, freshly brewed, ground coffee, but beans work best.

1½ cups milk

3 tablespoons coffee beans

4 extra large egg yolks

⅓ cup sugar

1 cup heavy cream, well chilled

4 oz. bittersweet chocolate, chopped

an ice cream maker or freezer-proof container

Serves 4–6

Put the milk into a heavy saucepan. Put the coffee beans into an electric coffee grinder and crack coarsely. Alternatively, put them into a dry dish cloth and crush with a heavy saucepan. Add to the saucepan and heat until the milk almost boils. Remove from the heat, cover, and leave to infuse for 15–20 minutes.

Put the egg yolks and sugar into a bowl and mix well. Strain the warm milk onto the mixture, stir well, then pour back into the saucepan. Stir over low heat until thick enough to coat the back of a wooden spoon—do not let the mixture boil or it will curdle. Remove from the heat, strain into a bowl, let cool, then chill. Put a bowl and whisk into the refrigerator to chill.

When ready to churn, put the cream into the chilled bowl and, using the whisk, whip until soft peaks form. Carefully stir into the coffee custard. Pour into an ice cream maker and churn until very thick. Add the chopped chocolate and churn until frozen. Eat immediately or store in the freezer. Alternatively, put the mixture into a freezer-proof container and freeze, stirring frequently, until very thick, then stir in the chocolate and freeze until firm.

maple pecan ice cream

An ice cream flavored with maple syrup instead of sugar is great with Brownies (page 59)!

1 cup pecans

1/3 cup maple syrup

1 1/4 cups milk

3 extra large egg yolks

5 1/2 oz. bittersweet chocolate, finely chopped

3/4 cup plus 2 tablespoons heavy cream, well chilled

a baking dish, well-oiled

an ice cream maker or freezer-proof container

Serves 4–6

Put the pecans (they can be whole or in large pieces) into the well-oiled baking dish, then add 1 tablespoon of the maple syrup and mix until the nuts are thoroughly coated. Toast in a preheated oven at 350°F for 10 minutes, then remove and let cool in the dish.

Put the milk into a heavy saucepan and heat gently. Put the egg yolks into a bowl, then stir in the remaining syrup. Pour in the warm milk and stir well. Pour the mixture back into the saucepan and stir gently over low heat until thick enough to coat the back of a wooden spoon—do not let the mixture boil or it will curdle. Remove the saucepan from the heat.

Put the chocolate into a large bowl and gently stir in the warm custard until smooth. Let cool, cover, then chill thoroughly. Put a bowl and whisk into the refrigerator to chill. When chilled, put the cream into the cold bowl and, using the whisk, whip the cream until soft peaks form. Stir in the cold custard. Pour into an ice cream maker and churn until thick. Add the toasted nuts and churn again until frozen. Eat immediately or store in the freezer. Alternatively, put the mixture into a freezer-proof container and freeze, stirring occasionally, until almost frozen, then stir in the nuts and freeze until firm.

intensely chocolate sorbet

A delicious recipe with just three ingredients—will your guests guess the spicy secret?

5 1/2 oz. bittersweet chocolate, very finely chopped

2/3 cup sugar

1 small dried red chile

an ice cream maker or freezer-proof container

Serves 4

Put the chopped chocolate into a large heatproof bowl. Put the sugar and 1 cup water into a heavy saucepan and heat very gently until the sugar has completely melted. Bring the mixture to a boil and boil for 2 minutes until slightly syrupy. Add the dried chile, then remove the saucepan from the heat, cover, and leave to infuse for 15 minutes.

If necessary, reheat the syrup until just warmer than your finger can stand, then strain the syrup onto the chocolate and stir gently until the mixture is smooth. Leave until cold, then pour into an ice cream maker and churn until frozen. Eat immediately or store in the freezer. Alternatively, put the mixture into a freezer-proof container and freeze, stirring frequently.

Variations If the Aztec flavoring doesn't appeal (the flavor is subtle and mysterious) replace the chile with a small bunch of fresh mint leaves. Slightly bruise the leaves with a rolling pin, then add to the hot syrup and leave to infuse as in the main recipe. Alternatively, use a vanilla bean split lengthwise, a broken up cinnamon stick, a large star anise, or even 1 tablespoon of your favorite coffee beans.

cones and wafers

chocolate ice cream wafers

1 cup plus 2 tablespoons all-purpose flour

a pinch of salt

½ teaspoon baking powder

scant ¼ cup unsweetened cocoa powder

1 cup sugar

1 stick plus 1 tablespoon unsalted butter, cut into small pieces

1 teaspoon vanilla extract

several baking trays, lined with nonstick parchment paper

Makes 14–16

Sift the flour, salt, baking powder, cocoa, and sugar into a food processor. Add the butter and vanilla and process until the dough comes together into a ball. Shape into a brick, 4 x 3 x 2 inches. Wrap in wax paper and chill until firm. Using a sharp knife, cut the dough into wafer-thin slices. Set apart on the trays and bake in a preheated oven at 400°F for 5–7 minutes until just firm and the edges are starting to color. Let cool for 2 minutes until firm enough to transfer to a wire rack.

Best eaten within 5 days. The dough can be kept in the refrigerator for up to 1 week or frozen for up to 1 month.

chocolate ice cream cones

Simple, really—and the perfect way to provide an extra dose of chocolate for the truly committed chocolate lover.

4 oz. bittersweet chocolate

8 ice cream cones

a pastry brush

several baking trays, lined with nonstick parchment paper

Makes 8

Put the chocolate into a heatproof bowl set over a saucepan of steaming but not boiling water and melt gently (do not let the base of the bowl touch the water). Using a pastry brush, brush the inside of the cones with the melted chocolate. Arrange on the baking trays and let set in a cool place (or the refrigerator in very hot weather).

chocolate baskets

Beaten egg whites are the basis for these crisp tuile baskets. The mixture must be spread thinly, baked until light brown, then quickly draped over an orange to give a basket shape. The tuiles can also be rolled up. Don't worry if the first couple you make are not perfect—you'll soon get the hang of it.

2 extra large egg whites

½ cup sugar

¼ cup plus 2 tablespoons all-purpose flour

4 tablespoons unsalted butter, melted and cooled

1 oz. bittersweet chocolate, very finely chopped

grated zest of 1 unwaxed orange

several baking trays, lined with nonstick parchment paper

Makes about 16

Put the egg whites into a spotlessly clean, greasefree bowl and, using electric or rotary beaters or mixer, beat until stiff peaks form. Beat in the sugar. Sift the flour onto the whites, gently fold it in using a large metal spoon, then fold in the cooled melted butter, chocolate, and orange zest.

Put a scant tablespoon of the mixture onto a prepared baking tray and spread thinly with the back of a spoon to make a 5-inch disk. Make another disk in the same way, then bake in a preheated oven at 350°F for 7–10 minutes until lightly browned. Continue making and baking 2 disks at a time.

Using a spatula, carefully lift each tuile off the tray and, while still hot, drape over an orange so it cools and sets in a basket shape. The hot tuiles can also be rolled around the handle of a wooden spoon to make thin, crisp, rolled-up tubes. If the tuiles become too cool to shape, return them to the oven for 1 minute to soften. Store in an airtight container.

Best eaten within 24 hours.

drinks

Chocolate was originally consumed as a frothy, intensely flavored, high-status drink for the well-off. More recently, chocolate drinks were thought of as a comforting bedtime treat—but now it's time for them to come in from the cold!

the finest hot chocolate

3 oz. bittersweet chocolate, broken into pieces

1 tablespoon sugar, or to taste

1 vanilla bean, split lengthwise

1¼ cups milk

⅓ cup heavy cream or whipping cream, whipped

freshly grated chocolate or unsweetened cocoa powder, for sprinkling

2 mugs, warmed

Serves 2

The ultimate hot drink—the best quality chocolate, a hint of vanilla, lots of frothy milk topped with whipped cream and grated chocolate. This is what chocolate lovers have been waiting for. Make sure the mugs or cups are warmed beforehand and, for a real treat, serve with Giant Double Chocolate Nut Cookies (page 67).

Put the chocolate pieces, sugar, vanilla bean, and milk into a small, heavy saucepan. Heat gently, stirring, until the chocolate has melted, then bring to a boil, beating constantly with a balloon whisk, until very smooth and frothy. Remove the vanilla bean.

Pour into warmed mugs, top with whipped cream and a sprinkling of freshly grated chocolate or cocoa, and serve immediately.

monsieur st disdiers' chocolate

1½ oz. bittersweet chocolate, finely chopped

2½ tablespoons sugar, or to taste

2 large pinches of ground cinnamon

½ vanilla bean, split lengthwise

4 cups, warmed

Serves 4

This French recipe was first recorded in 1692 and soon became a court favorite in England. I tasted it during an Easter chocolate celebration at London's Hampton Court Palace, where historians were on hand to describe how chocolate was prepared for King William III. Monsieur St Disdiers was the first Royal Chocolate Maker—the King enjoyed chocolate so much he installed a special chocolate kitchen in the royal apartments in 1699. Making the chocolate drink for the King was a job for an expert, and good chocolate makers were highly prized. The froth was very important—some cooks would add egg white to increase the volume of the froth. It is incredibly rich, so serve in small quantities.

Put 1¼ cups water into a heavy saucepan, bring to a boil, then remove from the heat and add the chocolate, sugar, and cinnamon. Using the tip of a small knife, scrape the seeds from the vanilla bean into the saucepan.

Using a balloon whisk, beat constantly for a few minutes, taking care not to splash the boiling liquid. When a good amount of froth has been created, pour the chocolate into warmed cups, then spoon the froth on top and serve.

john nott's wine chocolate

1¾ cups port

2 oz. bittersweet chocolate, grated

⅓ cup sugar, or to taste

1 teaspoon cornstarch

4 cups or mugs, warmed

Serves 4

At Syon House in Isleworth, England, the country house of the Dukes of Northumberland, the food historian Peter Brears prepared this drink created by the pastry cook John Nott at Syon in 1726. It sounds odd, but tastes delicious.

Put all the ingredients into a heavy saucepan and beat well. Bring to a boil, beating constantly, then serve.

hot spanish

Dip tall cinnamon sticks into melted chocolate, leave to set, then use to stir this special drink.

2 oz. bittersweet chocolate, broken into pieces

1 cup milk

1 tablespoon sugar

1 cinnamon stick

1¼ cups hot, strong black coffee

2 tablespoons brandy (optional)

2 curls of fresh orange peel

2 tall heatproof glasses, warmed

Serves 2

Put the chocolate, milk, sugar, and cinnamon into a small, heavy saucepan and heat gently, stirring constantly, until melted and smooth. Bring the mixture to a boil, beating constantly with a balloon whisk, then remove from the heat and beat in the coffee and brandy, if using. Remove the cinnamon stick.

Put the curls of orange peel into tall, warmed, heatproof glasses, pour over the hot mixture, and serve.

hot mocha

This is a truly classic coffee-chocolate combination. For best results, use freshly brewed coffee.

4 oz. bittersweet chocolate, broken into pieces

1 tablespoon sugar, or to taste

1¼ cups milk

2 cups hot, strong black coffee

½ cup heavy or whipping cream, whipped

4 large mugs, warmed

Serves 4

Put the chocolate, sugar, and milk into a small, heavy saucepan and stir over low heat until melted and smooth. Bring to a boil, beating constantly with a balloon whisk, then remove from the heat and beat in the hot coffee. Pour into warmed mugs, top with whipped cream, and serve immediately.

Variation

Iced Mocha Follow the recipe for Hot Mocha, but omit the cream. Make up the mixture of chocolate, sugar, milk, and coffee as given, then let cool and chill. Put the mixture into a blender, add 2 scoops (about 3 oz.) vanilla ice cream (optional) and blend briefly. Fill tall, chilled glasses with ice cubes, then pour over the mocha drink and serve immediately.

mail order sources and websites

Lake Champlain Chocolates
750 Pine Street
Burlington, Vermont 05401
Tel: 802-864-1807
www.lakechamplainchocolate.com
*Handmade chocolates made with
Callebaut chocolate from Belgium.
The Factory Shop also sells cocoa
and bars of their chocolate for
home baking. You can also see the
factory. Mail order available.*

**King Arthur Flour Baker's
Catalogue**
P.O. Box 876
Norwich, Vermont 05055-0876
Tel: 800-827-6836
www.kingarthurflour.com
*A catalog of everything the home
baker could ever need, everyday
and hard-to-find ingredients,
including good-quality chocolate
and cocoa, as well as equipment
and books. There's a cooking
school too. Write, phone, or shop
online, or visit the wonderful Baker's
Store in Norwich.*

Dean and Deluca
560 Broadway
New York NY 10012
Tel: 800-221-7714
*If you can't visit the store to buy
high-class chocolate supplies, write
or phone for a catalog.*

Sweet Celebrations
P.O. Box 39426
Edina, MN 55439-0426
Tel: 800-328-6722
Fax: 612-943-1508
www.sweetc.com
*An online and print catalog
featuring unique, ethnic, and
gourmet cookware and ingredients.*

Zingerman's Mail Order
620 Phoenix Drive
Ann Arbor, Michigan 48108
Tel: 888-636-8162
www.zingermans.com
*Gourmet foods store with a
discriminating mail order service.*

Williams-Sonoma
3250 Van Ness Avenue
San Francisco, CA 94109
Tel: 877-812-6235
Fax: 702-363-2541
www.williamssonoma.com
*Online and retail source for fine
baking products and equipment.*

**Hawaii Vintage Chocolate
Company**
1050 Bishop Street, Suite 162
Honolulu, HI 96813
Tel: 808-735-8494
www.hawaiianvintage.com
*Online source for the only
chocolate grown in America.*

Fran's Chocolates, Ltd.
1300 East Pike Street
Seattle, WA 98122-4020
Tel: 800-422-3726
Fax: 206-322-0452
www.franschocolates.com

Martha By Mail
PO Box 60060
Tampa, FL 33660-0060
Tel: 800-950-7130
www.marthabymail.com
Online and print catalog.

Chocosphere.com
Portland, Oregon
Tel: 877-992-4626
www.chocosphere.com
*Online source for fine chocolates
from around the world, including
kosher chocolate.*

Ghirardelli Chocolate Company
1111 139th Avenue
San Leandro, CA 94578-2631
Tel: 510-483-6970
Fax: 510-297-2649
www.ghirardelli.com
*Nationwide retail and mail-order
distributor of Ghirardelli Chocolate
Bars, Baking Chocolate, Chocolate
Beverages, Chocolate Gifts, and
Confections.*

Lindt USA
One Fine Chocolate Place
Stratham, NH 03885-0276
Tel: 603-778-8100
Fax: 603-778-3102
www.lindtusa.com
*United States-based distributor
of Lindt chocolates.*

**New York Cake & Baking
Distributor**
56 West 22nd Street
New York, NY 10010
Tel: 800-942-2539 /
212-675-2253
*New York's most beloved baking
ingredient and equipment retail
store. Call for a catalog
($5 shipping cost).*

**Scharffen Berger Chocolate
Maker, Inc.**
914 Heinz Avenue
Berkeley, CA 94710
Tel: 800-930-4528 /
510-981-4050
Fax: 510-981-4051
www.scharffenberger.com
*This American chocolate company
produces a high-quality selection
of richly flavored baking and
snacking chocolates.*

Chocolatesource.com
9 Crest Road
Wellesley, MA 02482
Tel: 800-214-4926
Fax: 781-237-1787
www.chocolatesource.com
*Online source for all chocolate
needs.*

Chocolates El Rey, Inc.
P.O. Box 853
Fredericksburg, Texas 78624
Tel: 800-357-3999
www.chocolate-elrey.com
*The source for chocolate made
from 100 percent Venezuelan
cacao—reputed to be the most
flavorful and aromatic in the world.*

index

conversion charts

Weights and measures have been rounded up
or down slightly to make measuring easier.

volume equivalents

american	metric	imperial
1 teaspoon	5 ml	
1 tablespoon	15 ml	
¼ cup	60 ml	2 fl.oz.
⅓ cup	75 ml	2½ fl.oz.
½ cup	125 ml	4 fl.oz.
⅔ cup	150 ml	5 fl.oz. (¼ pint)
¾ cup	175 ml	6 fl.oz.
1 cup	250 ml	8 fl.oz.

weight equivalents:

imperial	metric
1 oz.	25 g
2 oz.	50 g
3 oz.	75 g
4 oz.	125 g
5 oz.	150 g
6 oz.	175 g
7 oz.	200 g
8 oz. (½ lb.)	250 g
9 oz.	275 g
10 oz.	300 g
11 oz.	325 g
12 oz.	375 g
13 oz.	400 g
14 oz.	425 g
15 oz.	475 g
16 oz. (1 lb.)	500 g
2 lb.	1 kg

measurements:

inches	cm
¼ inch	5 mm
½ inch	1 cm
¾ inch	1.5 cm
1 inch	2.5 cm
2 inches	5 cm
3 inches	7 cm
4 inches	10 cm
5 inches	12 cm
6 inches	15 cm
7 inches	18 cm
8 inches	20 cm
9 inches	23 cm
10 inches	25 cm
11 inches	28 cm
12 inches	30 cm

oven temperatures:

225°F	110°C	Gas ¼
250°F	120°C	Gas ½
275°F	140°C	Gas 1
300°F	150°C	Gas 2
325°F	160°C	Gas 3
350°F	180°C	Gas 4
375°F	190°C	Gas 5
400°F	200°C	Gas 6
425°F	220°C	Gas 7
450°F	230°C	Gas 8
475°F	240°C	Gas 9